Sacred Strands is akin to studying [   ] tapestry. Lois Clymer shows how the many strands of history, science, astronomy, and more are interconnected with the biblical account of redemption. Each strand, in its own way, points to the masterful design and handiwork of the Master Weaver. This book is both an easy read and also one that will fill the reader with wonder and whet the appetite for further study.

— Brett R. Miller
Pennsylvania State Representative

In an age when we reject traditions and the wisdom of the ages, Lois Clymer reminds us that great truths—indeed, even a nugget of the greatest truth—were passed down and confirmed through many ancient traditions. The rediscovery of these ancient truths preserved through millennia inspires the imagination and reignites our wonder for our God.

— Randall L. Wenger
Chief Counsel, Pennsylvania Family Institute

The apostle Paul wrote to the church at Ephesus, "For God has allowed us to know the secret of his plan, and it is this: he purposes in his sovereign will that all human history shall be consummated in Christ, that everything that exists in Heaven or earth shall find its perfection and fulfilment in him" (Eph. 1:9–10, Phillips). The history of humanity is, after all, "Christ, His Story." In her book *Sacred Strands*, Lois Clymer masterfully weaves a tapestry of gospel truth, which spans the ages and identifies its Supreme Author. Her research demonstrates the veracity and the universality of God's plan for the redemption of mankind—a plan perfectly presented and preserved in the Holy Scriptures but evidenced, also, in the literature and folklore of ancient cultures, whose knowledge of God and His plan had become obscured. As Clymer aptly reveals in her work, even still "the heavens are telling of the glory of God; and their expanse is declaring the work of His hands" (Ps. 19:1, NASB). Don't miss the opportunity to take this uniquely focused exploration through history!

— **Michael Myers,**
Headmaster, Dayspring Christian Academy

While God often hides His footprints (Psalm 77:19), His fingerprints are found all over the universe and throughout human history. Lois Clymer has wonderfully traced God's fingerprints, all of which demonstrate and lead to His great act of redemption at the cross. This work will expand every reader's ability to bear a greater witness to the world about us that remains blind to God's fingerprints. *Sacred Strands* enlarges both our knowledge and faith.

— **Dr. Ron Susek**
President, Susek Evangelistic Association;
founder, FaithWalk Ministries International

This book promises to be a good apologetic on the theme of the story of the Redeemer in history. God has had a message for people since creation. There are many valuable clues down through the story of history that confirm this and throw light on the greatest event in all of history, when Jesus Christ the Redeemer gave His life to redeem sinful people who were under the curse of God. These indications of the Redeemer's sacrifice will help people to understand their opportunity to take advantage of God's offer of redemption.

— **Ken Fleming**
Author, *God's Voice in the Stars*

SACRED STRANDS

The Story of a **Redeemer**
Woven through History

BY

LOIS CLYMER

To my husband Jim for his help and
encouragement, and his deep faith in God

Table of Contents

Introduction

I magine a tapestry with the story of the world woven from the beginning of time. In this book we will discover the threads which will lead to the most important event of all history—the coming of the Sacred Promise, Jesus Christ, to redeem mankind.

These threads, the bits and pieces woven through history, tell of the promise of a Redeemer. We find this prediction of the Sacred Promise in the first chapters of Genesis in the Bible. We also find it in the constellations and in the ancient myths and stories and artifacts throughout all countries.

In the past three hundred years this message of a Redeemer has been disparaged by some. In the eighteenth century, several important philosophers and theologians began to question the validity of miracles. Genesis begins the story of a Redeemer and relates much early history. Nonetheless, a group of theologians called "higher critics" questioned if Genesis was a true historical account.

Modern archeology has done much to restore confidence in Genesis as true history. We will examine threads that support the fact of Genesis as real history. Some of these threads are bits of secular history, such as cuneiform tablets and artifacts; others are scientific theories such as the biological decay curve.

Some skeptics believe that Christianity is a religion simply copied from old pagan myths and mysteries. We see that thinking today in books such as *The Jesus Mysteries: Was the "Original Jesus" a Pagan God?* by Timothy Freke and Peter Gandy, published in 1999; and *The Da Vinci Code* by Dan Brown, published in 2003.

Can we prove that Christianity was not borrowed from pagan myths and mysteries? We can, by tracing the fascinating threads which show the story, the Sacred Promise, woven throughout history. The story of Jesus begins not in Bethlehem but at the beginning of man's time on Earth. Some of these threads are the myths, the constellations of the zodiac, and other astronomical signs. Perhaps the most amazing threads of all are the threads of the Shroud of Turin—the burial garment of Jesus Christ.

As we explore the threads, we will look at ancient history: the early ages of Sumer and Akkad, Egypt, India, and Israel; and then the early history of Greece, Rome, Persia, and China. We will examine how these people lived, how they dressed, what they believed, and how the story of a Redeemer is woven into their myths and foreshadowed in some of their religious practices, including their animal sacrifices.

Ancient history is considered to cover the period of the oldest discovered writings, the cuneiform of the Sumerians, beginning around 3000 BC; and since some historians also include the classical world of the Greeks and Romans, we will place the end of ancient history around 500 AD, at the beginning of the Middle Ages.

In this book we will center on the event which shook the world—the crucifixion and resurrection of Jesus Christ. Beginning with the earliest history, we will look for predictions of a Redeemer and parallels to what we have read in Genesis. Starting with the account in Genesis, we will trace the thread of the promise of a Redeemer, the Sacred Promise, through the stories and myths of human civilization.

Chapter 1

The Beginning of the Sacred Promise

Then Joseph could not control himself before all those who stood by him, and he cried,

"Have everyone go out from me." So there was no man with him when Joseph made himself known to his brothers. And he wept so loudly that the Egyptians heard it, and the household of Pharaoh heard of it. Then Joseph said to his brothers, "I am Joseph! Is my father still alive?" But his brothers could not answer him, for they were dismayed at his presence.

Then Joseph said to his brothers, "Please come closer to me." And they came closer. And he said, "I am your brother Joseph, whom you sold into Egypt.

And now do not be grieved or angry with yourselves, because you sold me here; for God sent me before you to preserve life." (Genesis 45:1–5)

Genesis Tells of the Sacred Promise

Genesis, of the Old Testament, contains in its early chapters the oldest written history that we have. Genesis begins with the creation of the world and all that is in it and ends with the well-known Bible stories of Joseph and his captivity in Egypt.

In Genesis 3 we find the first mention of the Sacred Promise—the story of a Redeemer. The story begins with the serpent tempting Eve to eat of the tree which was forbidden. Eve tells the serpent that God has said, "You shall not eat from it or touch it, lest you die" (v. 3). The serpent replies, "You surely shall not die!" (v. 4), and tells Eve that if she eats it, she will be like God. Eve eats of the fruit and gives it to her husband. When they heard the sound of the Lord God walking in the garden, they hid themselves. God called to the man, asking him where he was. Adam said, "I heard the sound of You in the garden, and I was afraid because I was naked; so I hid myself" (v. 10).

God replied, "Who told you that you were naked? Have you eaten from the tree of which I commanded you not to eat?" (v. 11). Adam then blamed Eve, and Eve blamed the serpent. God gave a punishment to the serpent, and to Adam and Eve, and sent them out from the Garden of Eden. To the serpent he said, "And I will put enmity between you and the woman, and between your seed and her seed; he shall bruise you on the head, and you shall bruise him on the heel" (v. 15). Charles Ryrie, in his study Bible, says the following regarding this verse: "Christ will deal a death blow to Satan's head at the cross, while Satan would bruise Christ's heel (cause Him to suffer)."[1] This verse is called the *protoevangelium*, meaning "first gospel." The seed of the woman refers to a virgin birth. In ancient times a birth was considered to come about because of the man's seed, so a birth from the seed of a woman would be a virgin birth.

Joseph Farah, in his book *The Gospel in Every Book of the Old Testament*, suggests that when Christ's heel was bruised, it may have been the natural result of crucifixion. In order to breathe, a victim of crucifixion needed to push his whole body up by the heel which was nailed to the cross, thereby creating a tremendous bruising of the heel.[2]

We find some of the following features in this story:

- Adam and Eve initially lived in a paradise (Garden of Eden), where they communed with God and had a body which would not die.

- Disobedience to God caused them to lose their immortality. They now had a body which would die.

- God promised that through the "seed" of the woman, Satan's head (his power) would be bruised, but this "seed" would be bruised by Satan in the heel. This "seed" is Christ.

We can find the symbolism used here, that of the "seed" struggling with Satan and bruising his head, while being bruised in the heel, throughout history. We can also find other remnants of the story—that of Satan tempting Adam and Eve, and their lost immortality and lost paradise.

Because Adam and Eve sinned after the serpent's temptation, they and their posterity lost both life in paradise and immortality. However, a "seed" was promised who would defeat the head of the serpent (Satan), even though this "seed" would suffer in the process.

Archeological finds have discovered several ancient clay drawings which represent the first part of this story—that of the serpent tempting Adam and Eve to eat of the fruit of the tree. One of these clay drawings shows a man and woman sitting beside a tree, one on each side of the tree, and each is reaching an arm toward the tree while behind the woman is a snake. This ancient art is described in and also featured on the cover of Bill Cooper's book *The Authenticity of the Book of Genesis*. This "temptation seal" shown there is an impression from a cylindrical seal. It dates back to around 2200 BC and today resides in the British Museum, where it is known as ME 89326.[3]

There is also a hint of this story in one of the oldest known writings, *The Epic of Gilgamesh*. This epic is the story of Gilgamesh's adventures and his fear of death and search for immortality. In his search for immortality he goes to inquire of his ancestor Upa-Napishtim (Noah), who is now sitting among the gods. At the end of the poem, when he is told the secret of immortality, a plant and a snake are involved: Gilgamesh retrieves the plant, but it is snatched away by the snake before Gilgamesh eats it. Gilgamesh is unable to acquire immortality. The epic of Gilgamesh will be covered in more detail in the next chapter.

The Constellations Show the Story of a Redeemer

In the constellations we see the symbolism of the ancient promise of a Redeemer, portrayed as the conqueror of the serpent. Here we see, in picture form, the seed of the woman who would bruise the head of the serpent while being bruised in the heel (Genesis 3:15).

The first-century historian Josephus credits Seth and his children with the invention of astronomy.[4] Jewish, Persian, and Arabian writers also say that the family of Seth (Adam, Seth, and Enoch) invented astronomy.[5]

Seth was the son of Adam; and Enoch was the great-great-great-grandson of Seth. Looking at the long lives of these three, we see that Adam, Seth, and Enoch would have spent three hundred years together. The long lives would have been an advantage for learning the cycles of the planets and stars. Enoch must have been a very godly man, as the Bible reports, "Enoch walked with God; and he was not, for God took him" (Genesis 5:24).

These very ancient men would have known that Adam lost immortality when he sinned and that a Redeemer had been promised—the conqueror of the serpent. We do not know what else God may have told the ancient men about this promise. This Redeemer, who would bruise the head of the serpent and thereby redeem man from the clutch of evil, would have been very important to them. It is certainly not surprising that they would have written the story in the sky, via the constellations. The constellations are formed of stars which do not, for the most part, resemble the symbol or figure for which they are named. Yet these same or similar constellations are found in all parts of the world, showing they had a common origin.

The ancient names of the stars, and the Roman and Greek myths which later became associated with the constellations, help to illustrate their message.

There are twelve major constellations which are on the ecliptic line, the circuit in which the sun appears to move through the sky in a year. Each major constellation is referred to as a "house," and each "house" also contains three minor constellations.

Virgo, Libra, and Scorpio, three major constellations, appear in sequence on the ecliptic line. They foretell the coming of the Redeemer. The constellation Virgo (see image), which has always been called the virgin, holds a branch in one hand and an ear of corn in the other. In her left hand, which holds the ear of corn, is Spica, one of the brightest stars in the heavens. Spica is a bluish, first-magnitude star, and its modern Latin name means "seed of corn." The branch held in the right hand is also found in other constellations such as Coma, Bootes, Hercules, Cepheus, Gemini, and Orion, and appears to have a meaning of "the one who comes." In the Old Testament, Jesus is referred to as the "branch" (Jeremiah 23:5).

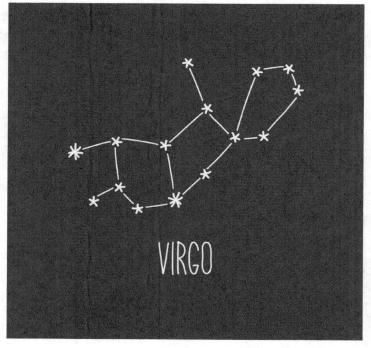

Virgo, the Virgin

One of the minor constellations in the house of Virgo is Coma, which in the old Denderah zodiac of ancient Egypt shows a woman holding a small child. Perhaps this constellation prefigures Mary and the Christ child.

The next sign along the ecliptic path is Libra, the scales (see image), suggesting a transaction to buy or redeem, showing the purpose of the Redeemer's coming. In Arabic, one of its star names means "purchase which covers." The earliest Persian planisphere pictured this sign as a man carrying a pair of scales in one hand and a lamb in the other.[6] A minor constellation in the house

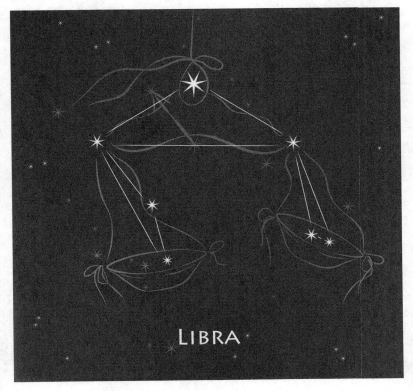

Libra, the Scales

of Libra is the Victim, which shows an animal being killed by Centaurus, the centaur. Underneath the centaur is the Southern Cross, another minor constellation of the house of Libra, which in our age can only be seen in the southern hemisphere.

Orhiuchus, the Serpent Holder and Scorpio, the Scorpion

In the next sign, Scorpio, the scorpion, we see the conflict in which the seed of the woman receives the wound in his heel, while bruising the head of the enemy, as foretold in Genesis 3:15. Ophiuchus, the serpent-holder, is located right above Scorpio on the planisphere. Above Ophiuchus is the constellation Hercules. Both Ophiuchus and Hercules are part of the house of Scorpio. They both show the hero crushing the head of the enemy while being bruised in the heel. The names of the stars emphasize this meaning. The Arabic and Syriac names for Scorpio mean "wounding him that cometh." The serpent, held by Ophiuchus, means "accursed"; and an Arab star name in Hercules means "head of him who bruises."[7] Ophiuchus is struggling with a serpent. His one foot is near the head of the scorpion, while his other foot is near the stinger tail of the scorpion.

We see the same illustration with Hercules. Hercules has one foot on the head of Draco, the dragon, while in his kneeling position his other foot is lifted, as if hurt.

These three major constellations—Virgo, Libra, and Scorpio—along with their minor constellations show in picture form the protoevangelium, the "first gospel" found in Genesis. The virgin gives birth to the Christ child. The "conqueror of the serpent" (Christ) is bruised in the heel while bruising the head of the evil one. The constellations Orion and Perseus also show this theme of "conqueror of the serpent." The other major constellations appear to include elements of the story of a Redeemer, although some may be referring to future events, and thus are more difficult to interpret.

Job Predicts the Redeemer

The setting of the book of Job is in the patriarchal period. This patriarchal period includes the first men mentioned in the Bible up to the time of Abraham, who was born around 2000 BC. There is no hint of the nation of Israel, while several references in Job refer to the early events recorded in Genesis such as creation, the fall, the flood, and the dispersion. Job mentions several constellations, including The Great Bear, the Pleiades, and Orion (Job 9:9).

Job predicts the coming Redeemer: "And as for me, I know that my Redeemer lives, and at the last He will take his stand on the earth. Even after my skin is destroyed, yet from my flesh I shall see God; whom I myself shall behold, and whom my eyes shall see and not another. My hearts faints within me!" (Job 19:25–27). Job, living around the time of 2000 BC, knew of the coming of the Redeemer. In the midst of his suffering, he had the hope of the Redeemer.

We have examined the promise of a Redeemer given in the first book of the Bible, Genesis. This Redeemer would restore to man what he had lost when he sinned. The symbolic language used is that of a seed of the woman bruising the head of the serpent while being bruised in the heel.

Chapter 2

Sumer and the Epic of Gilgamesh

The . . . land shattered like . . . a pot.

All day long the South Wind blew. . . .

Blowing fast, submerging the mountain in water,

Overwhelming the people like an attack,

No one could see his fellow,

They could not recognize each other in the torrent.

— The Epic of Gilgamesh,
Tablet 11, The Story of the Flood[8]

Sumer

One of the earliest civilizations archeologists have discovered is Sumer, located in Mesopotamia, along the Tigris and Euphrates rivers. Mesopotamia means "land between the rivers" (see map below).

The writing system of the Sumerians, called cuneiform, consisted of wedges pushed into soft clay and then hardened. The Sumerians used about six hundred symbols to represent sounds. Many clay tablets with cuneiform writing have been discovered in the past century in Mesopotamia. One of these discoveries is *The Epic of Gilgamesh*, considered to be one of the oldest pieces of literature of mankind. The poem tells about Gilgamesh, a king of Erech, which was also known as Uruk (see map). In Genesis 10:10, in referring to Nimrod, the writer says, "And the beginning of his kingdom was Babel [Babylon] and Erech and Accad and Calneh in the land of Shinar."

The name of Gilgamesh is found many places in Mesopotamian literature and cuneiform tablets. He is listed as the second king among the early kings of Erech, and as recently as April 2003 the tomb of Gilgamesh was unearthed in Iraq. Another person from this region was Abraham of the Bible, who was called of God to leave Ur (see map) and go to Caanan. This act was God's preparation for a line of people through whom the Redeemer would eventually come.

As one of the first kings of Erech, Gilgamesh is listed as having reigned 126 years around 2100 BC. Such a long reign and (assumedly lifespan) corresponds with the Genesis record of long lifespans before and after the flood, appearing to decrease with time after the flood. Noah lived 950 years, and his son Shem six hundred years, his grandson Arphaxad 438 years, and

Mesopotamia

Fertile Crescent

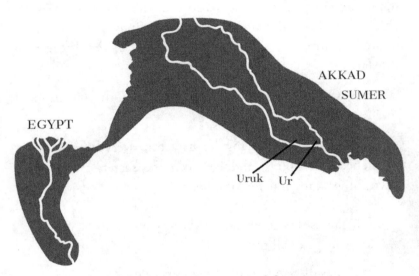

Map of the Fertile Crescent in Mesopotamia

then six generations later we find Abraham's father living 205 years around the time frame of 2100 BC. Abraham himself lived 175 years. These decreasing age spans have been plotted on a graph to show a biological decay curve. We see the long lifespans listed in Genesis compare with the long lifespan of Gilgamesh as listed in the tablet of the Sumerian kings. We also find the city of Gilgamesh's kingdom, Erech or Uruk, mentioned in Genesis 10:10.

The Epic of Gilgamesh

The Epic of Gilgamesh is a very long poem found on twelve clay cuneiform tablets. R. Campbell Thompson, an Assyriologist associated with the British Museum, made one of the first complete academic translations of the *Epic of Gilgamesh*, which contained almost two thousand lines. The following includes a summary and some actual lines of the Thompson translation:[9]

Tablet I. Of the tyranny of Gilgamesh and the Creation of Enkidu.

Gilgamesh begins by saying he has seen everything and has experienced all things, and has seen the secret, and handed down things known before the flood:

> [Gilgamesh]—he was the [Master] of wisdom, with knowledge of all things,
>
> He 'twas discovered the secret concealed. . . .
>
> (Aye), handed down the tradition relating to (things) prediluvian, . . .

Gilgamesh brags how he has built up the city and wall of Erech. But the people of Erech complain to the gods that Gilgamesh is a tyrant. So the gods create a rival for him, a wild man, Enkidu, who lives in the forests as an animal.

> E'en with gazelles did he pasture on herbage, along with the cattle

Drank he his fill, with the beasts did his heart delight
at the water.

Then the poem tells how a trapper was terrified when he came
face to face with this wild man. The wild man filled in the trapper's pits and helped the cattle escape his traps. The trapper's
father tells him to find Gilgamesh and then to bring back a
harlot to seduce him so that the wild man could return to Erech
and be civilized. The trapper does this, and the wild man returns
with the trapper and the harlot to Erech, bragging as he goes
that he can defeat Gilgamesh:

> I too, am mighty! Nay, I, forsooth [I] will (e'en) des-
> tiny alter—
>
> (Truly), 'tis he who is born in the desert whose vigour
> [is greatest!]

As they approach Erech, they tell Enkidu to look around and
see the great wall, to note how the people dress in fancy attire,
and to also note how each day is a festival with music and danc-
ing girls.

Tablet II. Of the Meeting of Gilgamesh and Enkidu.

The shepherds gather at the sight of Enkidu. He does not know
how to eat bread and he knows nothing of mead (beer). They
teach him to eat and drink and then put oil on his body, and
a garment like a man and "thus became human." He takes his
weapon and hunts jackals and lions for the shepherds:

> Hunted the lions, which harried the shepherds o'
> nights: and the jackals

Caught he. (So) he, having mastered the lions, the shepherds slept soundly.

Gilgamesh summons Enkidu to the House of Community. The people compare Enkidu with Gilgamesh as being equals. Then Enkidu and Gilgamesh have a mighty confrontation regarding the harlot. "They grappled and snorted(?) like bulls, (and) the threshold shatter'd; the (very) wall quiver'd as Gilgamesh and Enkidu grappled." At the end of the confrontation they become friends.

Tablet III. The expedition to the Forest of Cedars against Humbaba.

Gilgamesh is determined to go to the Forest of Cedars to destroy the evil Humbaba and then to cut down Cedars to bring to Erech. He wants Enkidu to go with him but Enkidu tries to dissuade him, saying how mighty Humbaba was:

Humbaba—his roar was a whirlwind,

Flame (in) his jaws, and his very breath Death! O, why hast desired

This to accomplish? To meet with Humbaba were conflict unequall'd.

Gilgamesh persuades him that it would be better to die in pursuit of a glorious enterprise than to die in peace. They have special weapons made, monstrous axes, and a bow and quiver. They take counsel with the elders and seek protection with the gods. Ninsun, mother of Gilgamesh begs a favor of the sun-god:

> Climb'd [she the stairway], ascended the roof, and [the parapet] mounted
>
> Offer'd her incense to Shamash. . .

Tablet IV. The arrival at the gate of the forest.

Enkidu becomes stricken with fear at the thought of combat with Humbaba, and he lies for twelve days with a sickness. Eventually, Gilgamesh persuades him by encouraging him not to be a coward, to forget death, and be fearful of nothing.

Tablet V. Of the fight with Humbaba.

> Stood they and stared at the Forest, they gazed at the height of the Cedars,
>
> Scanning the avenue into the Forest: (and there) where Humbaba
>
> Stalk'd, was a path, (and) straight were his tracks, and good was the passage.

The gods help by raising against Humbaba mighty tempests called Wind from the North, Wind from the South, Tempest, Storm Wind, Chill Wind, Whirlwind, and Evil Wind. Humbaba cannot go forward or backward. He begs Gilgamesh to spare his life, and he tells him that he will be his slave. Enkidu encourages Gilgamesh not to listen to him, and they cut off the head of Humbaba.

Tablet VI. Of the goddess Ishtar, who fell in love with the hero, but is spurned by Gilgamesh. She, in retaliation, sends the Bull of Heaven, but Gilgamesh and Enkidu manage to kill the bull.

Tablet VII. The death of Enkidu.

The gods decree that because Gilgamesh and Enkidu have slain Humbaba and killed the Bull of Heaven, one of them must die, and it is to be Enkidu. Enkidu lies for days with a sickness. Enkidu curses the harlot and then reverses his curse on the harlot and blesses her. In a dream he goes into the House of Darkness where the dead abide.

Tablet VIII. Of the mourning of Gilgamesh for Enkidu.

Gilgamesh mourns for his friend who has died:

> Unto me harken, O elders, to me, aye, me [shall ye listen],
>
> "Tis that I weep for my [comrade] Enkidu, bitterly crying." . . .
>
> Paced he backwards and forwards, tearing and casting his ringlets.

Tablet IX. Gilgamesh in terror of death seeks eternal life.

Gilgamesh has a fear of death and decides to seek the secret of immortality from Uta-Napishtim (Noah):

> Sorrow hath enter'd my heart; I fear death as I range o'er the desert,
>
> I will get hence on the road to the presence of Uta-Napishtim.

Tablet X. How Gilgamesh reached Uta-Napishtim.

Gilgamesh comes to the winemaker Siduri, and speaks to her regarding the death of his comrade and his quest for immortality:

> He whom I loved hath become alike the dust—[I,] shall I not, also,
>
> Lay me down [like him], throughout all eternity [never returning]?

The wine maker Siduri, tells him his quest is in vain, and he should enjoy life:

> Each day and night do thou dance and rejoice; (and) fresh be thy raiment. . . .
>
> Cherish the little one holding thy hand; be thy spouse in thy bosom happy.

However, she directs him to Ur-Shanabi, the boatman to Uta-Napishtim. Ur-Shanabi directs him to cut punting poles and they launch in his boat.

After a month and a half they reach the waters of death, and by using the punting poles do not allow the waters to touch them. Uta-Napishtim sees them coming and asks Gilgamesh, "Why is thy vigor all wasted?" Gilgamesh tells his story and asks regarding Death and Life.

Tablet XI. The Flood.

Gilgamesh asks Uta-Napishtim how he was able to stand in the Assemblage of Gods to ask for life everlasting, whereupon

Uta-Napishtim tells him he will give Gilgamesh the whole hidden story. He proceeds to tell the story of the flood. In a long speech he tells how the gods were moved to inflict the flood, how he was told to build a boat, how he was to build it, and how it was divided sevenfolds and the inside of it had nine compartments. He tells how he made it and about the huge amount of raw bitumen and pitch and oil he used. He tells how he had his kindred and family go up into the boat and also the cattle and beasts of the field at the stated time set by the god.

Uta-Napishtim said the wind and flood lasted six days and seven nights and then the sea calmed. On Mount Nimush the boat was lodged. On the seventh day he sent forth a dove which came back to him. He sent forth a swallow which came back to him. Then he sent forth a raven which did not come back to him. He then sent everything out and sacrificed a sheep and offered incense.

When Gilgamesh is about to be sent back, the wife of Uta-Napishtim asks what her husband can give to Gilgamesh so he could return to his land with honor. Uta-Napishtim says that none may know when he will die, nor can anyone avoid death, but he will disclose to him a thing that is hidden. He tells Gilgamesh about a plant that grows under the sea that would renew his youth.

Gilgamesh dives deep into the water to retrieve the plant. Taking the plant with them, Gilgamesh says they will take the plant to Erech and call it Greybeard-who-turneth-to-man-in-his-prime. Gilgamesh will eat it so that he can return to his youthful condition. They go on their way but stop to rest at a pool of cool water. A snake smells the fragrance of the plant, darts up, and snatches the plant. In sorrow, Gilgamesh and the ferryman continue on until they arrive at Erech. Gilgamesh tells the boatman Ur-Shanabi to go up onto the wall of Erech to admire the wall and the city, gardens, and the Temple of Ishtar.

In this epic poem, we find some biblical and extrabiblical correlation. We have clay tablets which mention the city of Erech and the long reign of Gilgamesh, which corresponds with information we find in the first chapters of Genesis. We have a story of a flood which was sent by God (gods) because of man's sins. In this story, a righteous man was told in a dream to build a boat. He took with him animals and his family, released a dove and raven, landed on Mount Nisir (near Mount Ararat), and sacrificed after the flood.

The epic itself suggests a lost immortality which Gilgamesh is searching for among his ancestors. These ideas show certain elements of the story in Genesis in which the man and woman, deceived by a snake, lose immortality.

The connections found in the Gilgamesh tablets suggest that there may be other important discoveries to be made from recent artifacts from the ancient ruins of Sumer.

Chapter 3

Akkad, Ur, and Abraham

"Is the decision final? Are we moving?"

"Yes," replied Terah.

Eliezer took a deep breath. Thoughts were whirling in his mind. Get the house on the market. Figure out the route they would take. Which of the cattle should they take with them and which should they sell? Buy tents. Which to do first? Eliezer went to see his realtor friend.

"Your house will sell easily. Beautiful large two-story house, lots of rooms, a chapel, a courtyard," the realtor told him.

Next Eliezer went outside the city walls and walked through their cattle sheds—sheep, goats, camels.

"I need a count," he told the herdsmen. When he got back to the house, Abraham found him.

"Eliezer, a ship is in the harbor with canvases and tents. We should go and examine them."

§   §   §

It may not have happened *quite* like this—but we do know that Abraham and his wife, his father, and Abraham's nephew did move from the city of Ur, which was a large, highly civilized city with large two-story houses. We also know that Abraham had large herds of cattle—sheep, oxen, donkeys, and camels. In Genesis 13:2 we read, "Now Abraham was very rich in livestock, in silver and in gold."

City of Akkad

As mentioned in the last chapter, the region of Sumer contained several city-states. The city of Akkad was the most powerful of these. Akkad was in the region where the Tigris and the Euphrates rivers are closest to each other. The ruler of Akkad was Sargon, who created what might be called the world's first empire. He brought order to the area, but he also brought cruelty and violence. Sargon founded Akkad around 2300 BC, and soon brought the rival Sumerian cities under his control by conquest. Obtaining power and assuming the title of king, he went on to conquer southern Mesopotamia and led military conquests to the east and north. (He was not, however, the first to unite the various city-states of Sumer under one rule. The king of Uruk, Lugalagery, had already accomplished this task, but on a much smaller scale.)

Sargon secured access to all the major trade centers by sea and by land. He maintained order through repeated military campaigns. The stability provided by his empire resulted in improved roads, irrigation policies, and wider trading.

The Akkadian empire even created a postal system. Clay tablets written in cuneiform were wrapped in outer clay tablets with the address of the recipient and the sender. When a person received one of these "letters," he would break open the outer clay tablet. Because postal systems seem like a modern invention, it is hard to imagine a postal system more than four thousand years ago.

After Sargon's death his two sons ruled a short time, followed by his grandson Narrm-Sin. When Akkad declined, the city of Ur took its place and became the dominant power in the area.

City of Ur

In its time Ur was a city of great size and wealth. Its position near the Persian Gulf allowed trade with countries as far away as India and helped Ur to accumulate wealth. The Code of Hammurabi is often referred to as the oldest law code, but this honor actually belongs to a code created by one of the kings of Ur. The Code of Ur-Nammu was written around 2050 BC on clay tablets in the Sumerian language. Earlier law codes are known to have existed and have been referred to, but their texts have not been found.

The Code of Ur-Nammu begins with a prologue in which the gods are invoked, and the king is said to have established order in the land. The pattern of laws in the code are such that if a crime was committed, certain punishment must follow. For offences such as murder, robbery, and rape, the punishment was death. Less serious crimes were punished by imprisonment or fines. The code stated that if a man committed a kidnapping, he was to be imprisoned and pay fifteen shekels of silver; if a man knocked out a tooth of another man, he would pay two shekels of silver. Laws also required that if the innocence of the accused person was proven, his accuser was to be punished instead.

When the ruins of Ur were excavated in 1922, many cuneiform tablets were discovered. Today one can visit the half-restored remnant of the very impressive ziggurat of Ur. The ziggurat was a three-tiered solid mass of mud brick which looked like a steeped pyramid. Located on its top was a small shrine for the worship of the moon god Nanna. The lowest part of the ziggurat was 210 feet by 150 feet and its height measured forty feet. On the northeast side were three great staircases, each of one hundred steps. From the second terrace, a single flight of steps led up to the top to the door of the little shrine. Perhaps this is similar to the stairway and shrine described in the *Epic of Gilgamesh* in our previous chapter, when Ninsun, mother of Gilgamesh, went to seek protection from the gods.

Another interesting feature of the third dynasty of Ur was the building of a 155-mile wall along the border of Sumer to keep out barbarian tribes. In 1750 BC the wall was breached by the neighboring kingdom of Elam. Ur was sacked and the last king was carried away as a prisoner. With the fall of Ur, the Sumerian empires came to an end.

Babylon

The area of Akkad is the area where the Babylonians began to dominate under their sixth ruler, Hammurabi the Great (1810–1750 BC). Hammurabi was famous for his detailed code of laws. The Babylonians controlled much of Mesopotamia for several hundred years. Then Babylon was overshadowed by Assyria, but later Babylon was revived and defeated the Assyrians. The

Babylonian and Assyrian men wore long coat-like garments and were bearded. The women wore a sleeved tunic and a shawl over their shoulders.

Nebuchadnezzar was another one of the famous kings of Babylon, who is mentioned in the Bible when the Israelites were carried away to Babylon. He built huge walls around the city and also built the Hanging Gardens, one of the Seven Wonders of the Ancient World. He built a huge ziggurat, the Temple of Marduk.

Wolfram von Soden was an important Assyriologist—one who studies ancient Mesopotamia, sometimes called the ancient Orient. Babylonia and Assyria are the primary cultures studied by Assyriologists. In his overview of the ancient Orient, von Soden pointed out that Babylonian prayers to their deities revealed thoughts closely related to the biblical psalms, especially regarding the relationship of humans to their deity. He suggested that the reason may be the extremely ancient religious heritage of the Semitic people, even though we see many differences.[10] The ancient Semitic-speaking people lived throughout the ancient Near East, including Mesopotamia. Perhaps that ancient religious heritage came from the first men of the Bible, the patriarchs.

Abraham

The Bible tells of the patriarch Abraham who came from the city of Ur, sometimes called Ur of the Chaldeans. The homes in Ur in the period that Abraham lived were comfortable and well-built; there were two-story houses with plenty of room for family, servants, and guests. In some homes there was a chapel in which the family god was worshipped.

In Genesis 11:31 we are told that Terah, Abram's father, took Abram (before God changed his name to Abraham) and his wife Sarai (before she became Sarah), as well as his grandson Lot, out of Ur to Haran, and that they settled there until Terah died at the age of 205. God then directed Abram to leave Haran and to go to a land God would show him. God promised him that in Abram's descendants all families of the earth would be blessed. This proclamation was the beginning of the line through which the Redeemer would eventually come.

Abraham traveled to Canaan, the Promised Land, and his son Isaac was born in his old age. God gives to Isaac the promise that he would bless him and multiply his descendants; the same promise is given to Isaac's son Jacob. Because of a famine in the land of Canaan, Jacob (later named Israel) and his children became sojourners in Egypt. Eventually they became slaves in Egypt, and Moses delivered them from slavery and led them to the Promised Land of Canaan.

The Israelites' time in Canaan was one of blessing and hardship. Prophets tried to keep them committed to God, but the hardships came when the people forsook the worship of God and eventually were taken captive. This story of the Old Testament contains many prophecies of the coming Redeemer. Jesus Christ was to be born from the line of Judah, a son of Jacob; when this event occurred, the story of the New Testament began.

Advice of an Akkadian Father to His Son

In the following passage found on a cuneiform tablet (c. 2200 BC), an Akkadian father encourages his son to live with integrity. He tells his son to "worship your god every day with sacrifice and pious utterance." The father encourages his son to return with kindness the one who does evil to him, not to covet, and to speak only good:

> Do not set out to stand around in the assembly. Do not loiter where there is a dispute. . . . Do not return evil to your adversary; requite with kindness the one who does evil to you, maintain justice for your enemy, be friendly to your enemy.

> Give food to eat, beer to drink, grant what is requested, provide for and treat with honor. At this one's god takes pleasure. It is pleasing to Shamesh, who will repay him with favor. Do good things, be kind all your days. . . .

> Do not marry a prostitute, whose husbands are legion, an Ishtar-woman who is dedicated to a god, a kulmashitu-woman. . . . When you have trouble, she will not support you, when you have a dispute she will be a mocker. There is no reverence or submissiveness in her. . . .

> Do not speak ill, speak only good. Do not say evil things, speak well of people. . . . Do not talk too freely, watch what you say. Do not express your innermost thoughts even when you are alone. What you say in haste you may regret later. Exert yourself to restrain your speech.

> Worship your god every day. Sacrifice and pious utterance are the proper accompaniment of incense. . . . Prayer, supplication, and prostration offer him daily.[11]

In these words we find some of the wisdom of God. We see in these moral teachings a similarity to the biblical moral code, even to the point of the father encouraging his son to return good for evil. These principles would influence Abraham who was to become the Father of a great people and through whom the promised Redeemer, the Sacred Promise, would come.

Following are some comparisons between the Akkadian father's advice and the Bible:

1.	Return evil with kindness	Matt. 5:39 Do not resist an evil person.
2.	Do good things, be kind	Eph. 4:32 Be kind to one another.
3.	Speak only good	Eph. 4:29 Let no unwhole-some word proceed from your mouth, but only such a word as is good.
4.	Restrain your speech	Prov. 13:3 The one who guards his mouth preserves his life.
5.	Worship your god every day	Ps. 1:1–2 Blessed is the man . . . [whose] delight is in the law of the LORD, and in His law he meditates day and night.

Were God's laws known to ancient man? We may think that ancient man did not know right from wrong, but when we compare this ancient Akkadian father's advice with biblical principles we see surprising comparisons. We don't know in what ways God spoke to ancient man, but it appears he did.

Chapter 4

Ancient Egypt and the Myth of Osiris

Imagine finding a mummy that is almost 2,500 years old. British archaeologist Howard Carter did just that when he discovered King Tut's tomb in Egypt in 1922. In 1905 Carter was convinced that the mummy was nearby when a small cup with the king's name on it was found. After years of searching, Carter stepped onto a sunken staircase that led to the tomb. Inside was King Tut's mummified body, along with five thousand burial objects.

The other tombs of the Pharaohs had been found and looted usually soon after the burial of the pharaoh. Why did it take so long for King Tut's tomb to be discovered? The reason may be that the pharaoh who came after King Tut had destroyed his temple and tried to erase his name from history. Other buildings had been placed by later pharaohs over top of King Tut's tomb.

The five thousand burial objects provide a look back into ancient history. The craftsmanship was exquisite, especially in the use of gold. The coffin in which Tut was buried was made completely of gold and is the most expensive coffin in the world. Among the objects in the tomb are a gold-covered two-wheeled royal chariot, ornate shields, and a jewel-covered replica of a flying serpent shaped like a collar. There is a statue of the dog Anubis, guardian of the underworld, carved from wood and painted black, with gold leaf in the insides of the ears, and on the eyebrows and collar. There are bird-hunting weapons similar to Australian boomerangs, and a huge collection of iron daggers. Some of the items are large, such as thrones and couches; and some are small, such as earrings and jewelry of all kinds.

The largest-ever King Tut exhibition opened in March 2018 in the California Science Center in Los Angeles and will be shown in ten major international cities for the following seven years.

Ancient Egypt

Ancient Egypt is another area studied by historians and archeologists. Since ancient Egypt was built along the Nile River, it was green and fertile even though it was surrounded by deserts. The Nile flooded every year and deposited rich soil along its banks. Farming along these banks was very productive. Farmers grew wheat and barley for bread and beer, and they grew flax for making linen. Egyptians used papyrus, a stiff paper made from the reeds of the papyrus plant, to make scrolls. They used hieroglyphs (symbols) for writing. People who could write were called scribes. These people became priests, and were also the ones who managed the rules and laws of the government. Religion was very important; priests held a revered status. Temples were built by pharaohs to uphold the gods, so resources were spent lavishly to build these temples and provide for the many rituals.

We know much about the life of ancient Egypt, partly because when the tomb of King Tut (Tutankhamen) was found in 1922, it had been untouched. Several rooms were found piled to the ceiling with things like carved wooden boats, statues of women grinding grain, and models of homes and their gardens.

Tutankhamen became a pharaoh at the age of eight or nine, but only lived to eighteen. He married a daughter of Amenhotep IV and his wife Nefertiti. Amenhotep lived during the eighteenth dynasty of Egypt, about 1553 BC. Unlike other pharaohs, he and Nefertiti chose to worship one god—the sun god—and no others. In fact, he destroyed references to other gods. He changed his name to Akhenaten, which means "pious servant of Aten." He was powerful in changing the religion of the country during his time, but when he died the people of Egypt returned to their old gods.

The Egyptians are famous for their pyramids. The Great Pyramid of Giza was built for Pharaoh Khufu and is one of the Seven Wonders of the Ancient World. This pyramid is as long as ten football fields and as tall as a forty-story building. It is a mystery how these pyramids were built, but obviously the Egyptians had great mathematical and building skills.

Myth of Osiris

The Egyptians were very religious. The ancient Greek historian Herodotus tells us that the Egyptians "are religious to a higher degree than any other people."[12] The gods of ancient Egypt were seen as creators and sustainers of life and order. They had brought order out of chaos and each person was expected to uphold the principle of harmony and truth (called *ma-at*). In this way, each individual would align himself with the gods against the forces of darkness and assure entrance into life after death.

The myth of Osiris was one of the most important myths of ancient Egypt. Osiris was seen as a dying and resurrecting god who brought salvation; he was sometimes depicted as the constellation Orion. The story line of the myth has many variations, and it appears that the religious ideas represented by the myth were more important than the details of the story. There are three major parts to the myth. The first is the death of Osiris caused by his brother Set and his subsequent restoration by his wife (or sister) Isis. The second is the birth of Horus, and the third is the conflict between Horus and Set.

Osiris is viewed as a primeval king of Egypt who taught the people how to plant crops and gave them laws and moral instruction which brought order to life in Egypt. His brother Set became jealous of his power and decided to kill him. One version says the brother built an elaborate and ornamental coffin, and at a party he hosted asked each of the guests to lie in the box. He stated that whoever fit in the coffin would own it. When Osiris lay down in the box, Set slammed the lid, sealed it, and put the coffin in the Nile River. Eventually it reached the town of Byblos, where a tree grew around the coffin. The tree was cut down and became a pillar in the palace, with the coffin still inside the tree with the dead Osiris. Set then took over the throne and became king.

Isis, the wife or sister, hunts for Osiris, eventually finds him and brings his body back home. She miraculously becomes pregnant with their son, Horus, sometimes by a flash of lightning and sometimes by a kite flying over her. She hides Horus from Set, but while she is in hiding, Set discovers the body of

Osiris, hacks it into fourteen pieces and scatters the pieces over the whole region.

Isis and her sister Nephthys hunt for the pieces of Osiris, and eventually find them and restore Osiris to life. Because he can no longer rule on Earth, Osiris becomes lord of the underworld.

The second part of the myth involves the birth and childhood of Horus. Isis hides Horus in a thicket of papyrus in the Nile Delta. Horus is a vulnerable child and the myths give him various ailments; most commonly, the child is bitten by a snake sent by the evil Set. During Horus's childhood, Isis is a devoted mother.

The third part of the myth involves a great conflict between Horus and Set. The conflict is seen as a divine struggle, usually characterized as a struggle between good and evil, with Set being the evil power. In some of the myths Horus, after a struggle lasting many years, becomes victorious.

The tale of Osiris was important to the people because it represented the concept of life after death. It was used in funeral texts, and Osiris was celebrated in festivals. The Egyptians had an annual celebration in which the ark of Osiris was borne by the priests, in a procession which traveled from Osiris's main temple to the tomb site. His death was mourned and his rebirth celebrated.

Osiris as Orion

Osiris is sometimes equated with the constellation Orion.[13] Orion, called The Glorious One, means "coming forth as light." On the planisphere he is shown as stepping on Lepus, the Hare, who is the enemy. The old Persian planisphere shows a picture of a serpent instead of a rabbit.[14] This constellation is a representation of the Sacred Promise as found in the Genesis story of Adam and Eve, in which the promised seed would bruise the head of the serpent (Genesis 3:15).

Some historians have traced the pagan religions to the constellations of the zodiac, but did not see meaning in the constellations. Christian writers such as Frances Rolleston and Joseph Seiss, however, feel that these themes of the constellations which we find among the pagan myths and mysteries come from the ancient truth which man was familiar with—that of the prediction of a woman-born conqueror of the serpent. In Genesis we find that after the fall of man God told the serpent (Satan) that the seed of the woman would bruise his head, but that he (the serpent) would bruise his heel.

Christian historians see in the pagan myths elements and symbols of the Genesis "conqueror of the serpent" flowing down through history, even though the revelation has been corrupted by many of the pagan ideas and practices. Some of the elements of the Sacred Promise which we see in the myth of Osiris are the miraculous birth of Horus, the serpent biting Horus, the struggle between Horus and Set (representing evil), and the bringing of immortality.

The Christian historian and philosopher Andrew Ramsay, in looking at the ancient myths, finds "traces that appear in all Religions of a Nature exalted, fallen, and to be repaired again by a Divine Hero."[15] These words echo the stories in Genesis of the fall and subsequent promise of a Redeemer.

Chapter 5

India and the Avatar Krishna

In 1856 a group of British railroad engineers were laying tracks through the Indus River Valley, in what is now Pakistan. As they searched for stone to lay around the railroad tracks to drain water from the path of the train, they discovered bricks which seemed very old—and all made exactly alike. Eventually the engineers realized that the bricks were part of one of the earliest civilizations in history.

The early people of India lived on the banks of the Ganges and Indus rivers. The Indus Valley civilization flourished for more than a thousand years, going into decline around 1500 BC; there is some evidence they were invaded by nomadic warriors. Archaeologists have discovered more than fifteen hundred settlements along the Indus River. The two largest which have been found are Harappa, named after a nearby village; and

Mohenjo Daro, which literally means "hill of the dead." These were expertly planned cities with a grid of wide, straight streets. Thick walls surrounded the cities. Sturdy brick houses were built, and had as many as three floors. Some had bathrooms and toilets connected to a sewer system. The houses were built around a court with a well.

These settlements had an irrigation system for growing wheat and barley. There is also evidence that they had sheep, cattle, and goats. They had a highly advanced knowledge of mathematics and a complex system of weights and measures. There is also evidence of musical instruments, toys, games, and pottery. They must have practiced some form of dentistry, as there are some gravesites containing the bones and teeth of people whose teeth had been drilled. Thousands of clay tablets show they had a writing system.

India

There were a group of people called the Dravidians who lived in northern India. They were later invaded by groups such as the Aryans and were pushed down into southern India.

The religion of the people of ancient India was Hindu. Their sacred scriptures were the Vedas. The prejudices of the different groups of people in India led to the development of a "caste system," creating four major ranks of people. Because it was very difficult, if not impossible, to move from one rank to another, people stayed in the caste they were born in. The highest rank was the Brahmans, or priests. Next were the Kshatriyas, the warriors and government administrators. Then came the Vaisyuas, the farmers and craftsmen. The lowest caste was the Sudras, who were the unskilled laborers.

The caste system has survived through the years. Modern India is attempting to undo the prejudices of the caste system, especially against the lowest group of people so that they can have better lives.

Hinduism and Buddhism

Both Hinduism and Buddhism originated in the Indian sub-continent. The founder of Buddhism was born into a Hindu family as a prince who eventually became the Buddha. Before developing his own path, he went to Hindu gurus and practiced under their guidance.

One of the reasons Buddhism gained popularity in India is because the Buddha ignored the caste structure and admitted anyone from any class. Although differing and frequently rejecting of each other, both Hinduism and Buddhism have many similarities and have influenced each other. A thousand years after Buddha died, the Vedic Hindu tradition accepted Buddha as an incarnation of Vishnu.

Hinduism and Buddhism share some similarities. Both emphasize the illusory nature of the world, with desire as the root cause of suffering. Both emphasize the spiritual practice of meditation, concentration, and mindfulness. Both believe in karma, the cycle of births and deaths and the transmigration of beings and rebirth. Both emphasize the importance of compassion and nonviolence toward all living things. Yoga is a Hindu tradition written long before the emergence of Buddhism, but Buddha practiced various forms of yoga.

There are some differences. Hinduism believes in the supremacy of the Vedas, but Buddhists do not believe in the Vedas or any Hindu scripture. Buddhism does not believe in the first cause or the creator God, while Hinduism believes that Brahma is the first of the gods in the Hindu triumvirate—the three gods (Brahma, Vishnu, and Shiva) who are responsible for the creation, upkeep, and destruction of the world. Brahma brought all things into being. Vishnu is the preserver god and has important incarnations, such as Krishna.[16]

Krishna

In the Hindu religion, an avatar is a manifestation of a deity in human form. Krishna is worshipped as the eighth avatar of the god Vishnu. He is the god of compassion, tenderness, and love in Hinduism and is highly revered among Indian divinities. Krishna became the focus of numerous sects, which over the centuries have produced much religious poetry and art.

Krishna was born into an Indian clan sometime before the fifth century BC; Devaki was his mother. Because of a prophecy that the king would be killed by a child of Devaki, the king tried to kill all of Devaki's children. Krishna was smuggled across the Yamuna River, where he was raised by a cowherd leader named Nanda. As a child he was known for mischievous pranks. He is pictured with blue-colored skin.

Two sculptures of Krishna still exist in one of the oldest pagodas in India. One sculpture represents Krishna trampling the crushed head of the serpent, while the other shows a poisonous reptile encircling the deity and biting his heel.[17] These sculptures illustrate the protoevangelium, the Genesis story with its symbolism of the man (the seed of the woman) who is bit on the heel by the serpent (Satan) while the man crushes the head of the serpent. It can be difficult to interpret the beliefs and myths of ancient people. Sometimes their symbols can tell us more than their words can. The symbolism of these Indian sculptures, which shows a similarity to the story and symbols given us in Genesis regarding the promised Redeemer, makes one think that some of the beliefs of the Hindus may have come from truths known by ancient men, as explained in the first chapters of Genesis. We see in the ancient Hindu religion a belief in a creator God and also the belief in the incarnation of a deity in human form (avatar).

Chapter 6

Ancient Israel and the Prophets

A t the Seder the youngest child asks the following questions:

1. On all other nights we eat either bread or matzah; on this night, why only matzah?

2. On all other nights we eat herbs or vegetables of any kind; on this night why bitter herbs?

3. On all other nights we do not dip even once; on this night why do we dip twice?

4. On all other nights we eat our meals in any manner; on this night why do we sit around the table together in a reclining position?

The rest of the participants at the Seder answer:

> We were slaves to Pharaoh in Egypt, and God brought us out with a strong hand and an outstretched arm. And if God had not brought our ancestors out of Egypt, we and our children would still be subjugated to Pharaoh in Egypt. Even if we were old and wise and learned in Torah, we would still be commanded to tell the story of the Exodus from Egypt. And the more we talk about the Exodus from Egypt, the more praiseworthy we are.
>
> —from a *Guide to the Seder*[18]

This commemoration of the Passover, which happened more than 3,500 years ago, is still observed by many Jews.

Ancient Israel

We met Abraham in chapter 3. To recap: Abraham was from the city of Ur. He left Ur when God directed him to go to the land of Canaan and told him that in his descendants all families on Earth would be blessed. Canaan was the name of a large and prosperous country located in the Levant region of present-day Lebanon, Syria, Jordan, and Israel. Abraham's family was the beginning of the line through which the Redeemer would eventually come. Abraham had a son Isaac; and Isaac had a son Jacob whose name was changed to Israel. Israel had twelve sons, whose descendants became the Israelites.

In the Bible we read the story of how the Israelites became enslaved in Egypt and fled Egypt under the leadership of Moses and eventually settled in Canaan, later called Israel. For a while the Israelites were ruled by judges until their first king, Saul. King David and his son Solomon followed. King Solomon built a magnificent temple. After the death of Solomon the kingdom was split, into a northern kingdom which retained the name Israel and a southern kingdom called Judah. In the Old Testament we read the stories of the Israelites and also the messages of the prophets to the people. These prophets admonished the people, and their prophecies sometimes included the promise of a Redeemer.

Prophecy is always more clearly understood when it has been fulfilled. We will examine some of these prophecies, beginning with Moses.

Moses

When the Israelites were slaves in Egypt, Moses attempted to persuade Pharaoh to let the people go. When he refused, God brought plagues on the Egyptians. The last plague was the death of all the firstborn. In order to protect the Israelites, Moses instructed them to sacrifice a lamb and sprinkle the blood on the lintel and doorposts of each house. When the angel of death would see the blood on the doorposts, he would pass over that house and not kill the firstborn. This event was the first Passover, which the Jews continue to celebrate each year. The Passover foreshadows (predicts) Christ's death on the cross. Significantly, when Jesus died on the cross, it was during the time of the preparation for the Passover.

Moses prophesied of the coming Redeemer: "The LORD your God will raise up for you a prophet like me from among you, from your countrymen, you shall listen to him" (Deuteronomy 18:15).

Isaiah

Isaiah, one of the four major prophets, lived eight centuries before the coming of Jesus. He lived at the time Assyria was threatening the southern kingdom of Judah. Isaiah spoke many prophecies concerning the coming Redeemer; and Joseph Farah, in *The Gospel in Every Book of the Old Testament,* shows that we can even see the gospel message spelled out in Isaiah's writings:[19]

- Everyone has fallen short. "For our transgressions are multiplied before You, and our sins testify against us; for our transgressions are with us, and we know our iniquities" (Isaiah 59:12).

- Sin separates us from God. "But your iniquities have made a separation between you and your God, and your sins have hidden His face from you, so that He does not hear" (Isaiah 59:2).

- The Redeemer has taken our sins upon Himself. "All of us like sheep have gone astray, each of us has turned to his own way; but the LORD has caused the iniquity of us all to fall on Him" (Isaiah 53:6).

- We must seek Him and call on Him for salvation. "Seek the LORD while He may be found; call upon Him while He is near" (Isaiah 55:6).

The book of Isaiah contains some amazing prophecies of the birth of Jesus. "Therefore the Lord Himself will give you a sign: Behold, a virgin will be with child and bear a son, and she will call His name Immanuel" (Isaiah 7:14); "For a child will be born to us, a son will be given to us; and the government will rest on His shoulders; and His name will be called Wonderful

Counselor, Mighty God, Eternal Father, Prince of Peace" (Isaiah 9:6); "Then a shoot will spring from the stem of Jesse, and a branch from his roots will bear fruit" (Isaiah 11:1). Isaiah also describes the suffering of Christ:

> He was despised and forsaken of men, a man of sorrows, and acquainted with grief; and like one from whom men hide their face, He was despised, and we did not esteem Him. Surely our griefs He Himself bore, and our sorrows He carried; yet we ourselves esteemed Him stricken, smitten of God, and afflicted. But He was pierced through for our transgressions, He was crushed for our iniquities; the chastening for our well-being fell upon Him, and by His scourging we are healed. (Isaiah 53:3–5)

In the New Testament we read the story of Jesus teaching in the synagogue, reading from the book of Isaiah, "The Spirit of the Lord is upon Me, because He anointed Me to preach the gospel to the poor. He has sent Me to proclaim release to the captives, and recovery of sight to the blind, to set free those who are downtrodden, to proclaim the favorable year of the Lord." When Jesus finished reading, he said to those listening, "Today this Scripture has been fulfilled in your hearing" (Luke 4:18–19, 21).

Micah

Micah was a prophet in the same time as Isaiah, when the northern kingdom was suffering because of their sins. He prophesied where the Messiah (Redeemer) would be born.

When the wise men came to Herod to ask the location of the newborn king of the Jews, Herod asked the chief priests and scribes where this child would be born. They quoted Micah 5:2 when giving the place of his birth: "But as for you, Bethlehem Ephrathah, too little to be among the clans of Judah, from you One will go forth for Me to be ruler in Israel. His goings forth are from long ago, from the days of eternity" (cf. Matthew 2:6).

Psalms

The book of Psalms is a collection of poems used as a hymnbook for the Hebrew people. The psalms often have double meaning—they tell the author's experiences while relating a prophecy of which the writer may be unaware, showing the divine inspiration.

David Limbaugh, in *Finding Jesus in the Old Testament,* explains how the Old Testament is revealed by the New Testament. Without the New Testament, we would not understand the progressive revelation we find in the Old Testament; but, when we connect the dots of the promises and covenants from God beginning in the first book of the Old Testament (Genesis) with the experiences of the Israelites and the teachings of their prophets, we find a unified message fulfilled by the New Testament. Limbaugh quotes Augustine as saying "The New Testament is in the Old concealed; the Old is by the New revealed."[20]

Following is a list of messianic prophecies which we find in the Psalms, followed by the reference showing their fulfillment in the New Testament:[21]

- Psalm 22:1: God would forsake Him. (Matthew 27:46)
- Psalm 22:7–8: He would be mocked. (Luke 23:35–39)
- Psalm 22:16: His hands and feet would be pierced. (John 20:25–27)

- Psalm 22:18: They would cast lots for His clothes. (Matthew 27:35–36)
- Psalm 34:20: None of His bones would be broken. (John 19:32–33)
- Psalm 35:19: He would be hated without cause. (John 15:25)
- Psalm 40:7–8: He would come to do God's will. (Hebrews 10:7)
- Psalm 41:9: He would be betrayed by a friend. (Luke 22:47)
- Psalm 45:6: His throne would be forever. (Hebrews 1:8)
- Psalm 110:4: He would be a priest forever, according to the order of Melchizedek. (Hebrews 7:17)

The Israelites had a role given by God of helping to usher in, from within their nation, the Messiah—the promised Redeemer who would bless all peoples.

Chapter 7

Greece and the Hero-gods Perseus, Asclepius, and Orion

One Thanksgiving our family vacationed in Alaska. Around midnight one night, we went to the top of a ski area to see if we could view the aurora (northern lights). We were fortunate that night and witnessed a fabulous show. Streaks of green, pink, yellow, and white moved across the sky, sometimes pulsating and moving, sometimes looking like curtains folded into the sky. Such magnificence! At one point the curtain seemed to open, and there was the constellation Orion, looking as regal as could be, the three stars in his belt shining brightly.

Orion is one of the most familiar of the constellations. We can pick out the many bright stars that form him—the

bright stars in his belt, and then the two bright stars near his
shoulders, and another two marking his feet or legs. Orion
is certainly a magnificent constellation. When Orion is up,
he dominates the southern sky. No other constellation has so
many bright stars, five of the second magnitude and two of
the first magnitude. The first-magnitude stars include reddish
Betelguese in his left shoulder and the bluish white Rigel in
his right foot.

The Constellation Orion

The Beginning of Greece

The earliest European civilization began on the island of Crete with the Minoan civilization. The capital at Knossos had a grand palace, and the Minoan craftsmen were famous for their pottery and buildings. The walls of the palace room were decorated with large murals, some of which depicted the sport of bull leaping, showing men catapulting over bulls. They were also expert shipbuilders, and these ships carried their pottery and crafts to areas such as Egypt. The civilization came to an end around 1400 BC, possibly because of a nearby volcanic eruption. The Mycenaeans greatly admired the Minoans and took their ideas to the mainland, which became known as Greece.

Mycenae, a city on the southern tip of Greece, became the center of the first Greek civilization. In time, the Greek civilization shaped much of Europe through its art, education, and government.

Perseus

One of the most beloved and admired of all the hero-gods of mythology was Perseus. He was the son of the god Zeus, who impregnated the mortal (human) Danae with a shower of gold. When he was born, he and his mother were put into a chest and cast into the sea. The gods directed that they be rescued by fishermen on the coast of Cyclades and treated with kindness by the king of the area.

Perseus had great wisdom and courage. He was sent to kill the Medusa by King Polydectes of Seriphus. The Medusa was one of the ugly Gorgon sisters who had snakes for hair. Anyone who ever looked at these snakes would immediately be turned to stone. To equip him for the task, Pluto lent him his helmet, which had the power to make the wearer invisible. Mercury gave him wings for his feet, and the goddess Athena gave him a highly polished shield, which he used as a mirror so that he was able to approach the Medusa without directly looking at her. When he cut off the head of the Medusa, the winged horse Pegasus sprang from her body. Perseus climbed upon Pegasus, and as he headed home he heard a woman's screams and was just in time to rescue Andromeda.

Young Andromeda, the daughter of King Cepheus and Queen Cassiopeia, was so beautiful that her mother had boasted that her daughter was more beautiful than the sea nymphs. The sea nymphs were goddesses and did not like being compared to a mortal. They had complained to the god Neptune, who was the highest sea god. Neptune sent out a sea monster who devoured the subjects of the kingdom of King Cepheus and Queen Cassiopeia. The sea monster was so ferocious that no one could kill him. King Cepheus was told by the gods that the only way to rid themselves of the monster was by sacrificing his daughter Andromeda. So Andromeda was chained to a rock to await her fate. After a time, the sea monster emerged and approached Andromeda.

But just as the sea monster neared Andromeda, Perseus appeared on his winged horse, Pegasus. Asking Andromeda to become his wife, he killed the sea monster and freed Andromeda. The two flew off on Perseus' winged horse. They lived happily for many years and their descendants became great kings. Perseus, by various miraculous powers, changed governments and rulers and returned to bless the countries that honored him.

Perseus is one of the many figures to which the Greeks attached one of the constellations. Perseus is one of the decans or minor constellations of the sign Aries, the Lamb or Ram. Perseus is pictured on the planisphere as an armed man holding a head with serpents (the Medusa). Medusa has a principal star in the head called "Al Ghoul" or "Algol," meaning "the evil spirit."[22]

The myth is the story of a god-man who "bruises the head of the serpent." Out of devotion to his king, Perseus seeks to destroy the evil Gorgon. He kills the sea monster. He breaks the bonds of Andromeda and makes her his wife. He goes forth to countries far and near, punishing and expelling tyrants.

Asclepius

Asclepius (also called Ophiuchus, the Serpent Holder) was held to be one of the worthiest gods. It was to him that the great Socrates, during his last hours, directed his followers to sacrifice a rooster.

Asclepius was worshipped throughout Greece, and many towns claimed the honor of his birth. He was a son of the god Apollo and the mortal Coronis. Known as a physician and healer, he was the god of medicine in ancient Greek religion. The rod of Asclepius, a snake entwined staff, is still a symbol of medicine today.

The centaurs were half-man and half-horse. The first centaurs were born from a cloud that their father, a god, had married, mistaking it for a goddess. The centaurs lived without law and ran over fields, trampling crops and destroying everything. They were hated by both the gods and men. But there was one centaur, Chiron, who was kind and wise and fond of children. Chiron was famous as the greatest teacher in Greece. People brought their sons to him in his cave, so he could train and teach them. He taught them sports and hunting and how to use herbs for medicine. One day Apollo brought his little son, Asclepius, to Chiron to raise the boy and to teach him all things.

Asclepius grew rich and famous, and as time went on he grew so skilled in medicine that he could even bring the dead back to life. The gods complained about this power of Asclepius, and eventually Zeus hurled a thunderbolt at him. Nothing was left of Asclepius but a heap of ashes, but Zeus placed him among the stars.

Asclepius, the serpent-holder, is a familiar constellation of the house of Scorpio, which also includes the Serpens (serpent) and Hercules. On the planisphere he is shown as a human figure grasping the serpent and stepping on the scorpion. With one foot lifted from the scorpion's tail as if hurt, he is in the act of crushing the scorpion's head with the other foot. What better picture could one find of the protoevangelium, in which the seed of the woman is described as bruising the head of the serpent while being bruised in his heel?

In Asclepius we see a "god-man" who was a matchless healer and physician who raised the dead. His symbol was a staff entwined with serpents. He was killed by a thunderbolt, but raised up to immortality among the stars.

Orion

As with most of the ancient myths, there are various versions of the story of Orion. Here is one: Orion was very powerful; he was strong and handsome, and was a great hunter. He fell in love with Merope on the island of Chios, and her father agreed to the marriage if Orion would first rid the island of all dangerous beasts. Orion did so, but Merope's father refused to let the marriage take place. In a drunken stupor, Orion forced himself on Merope; and her father in anger blinded Orion. Orion then traveled to the East to regain his sight from the sun god. After regaining his sight, Orion landed in Crete and fell in love with Artemis. He boasted that he was able to kill all animals, and the gods sent a gigantic scorpion, which bit Orion on his heel and killed him.

Asclepius the serpent-holder, who was a great healer, was called, and was able to bring Orion back to life. When Pluto, god of the dead, heard the news, he was worried. What would happen to his kingdom if people could be brought back to life? When he told his brother Jupiter about this problem, Jupiter sent a thunderbolt and killed Orion and Asclepius. After their deaths, they were put in the sky. Because Orion and Scorpio were put in opposite parts of the sky, when Scorpio rises in the sky, Orion sets below the horizon. Orion and his two dogs, Canis Major and Canis Minor, as well as the hare Lepus, are found in the winter sky. In the summer sky we can find Scorpio and Asclepius, the serpent-holder.

Orion, a well-known constellation, is part of the house of Taurus, the bull. His Hebrew name means "coming forth as light." A star on his shoulder means "the branch coming," and a star on his foot means "the foot that crusheth." This constellation is mentioned in the biblical book of Job as being so invincible no one can unloose its bands (Job 38:31). Orion is also mentioned in the book of Amos (5:8). Orion's figure on the planisphere is that of a giant hunter with a club in his right hand and in his left hand the skin of a slain lion. His left foot is in the act of stepping on the head of the enemy.[23]

In Orion we see another "god-man," a great hunter pictured holding the head of a slain lion. He was stung by the scorpion in the heel and died. This story in the stars is another illustration of the protoevangelium, the allegory of the seed of the woman who would crush the head of the serpent but be bruised in the heel.

Asclepius, Hercules, Perseus, and Orion are examples of the "god-man" or "conqueror of the evil one." We find these four in the constellations and in the ancient myths. In pictorial form, they represent the allegory of the promised Redeemer. They are four more threads added to the story of the Sacred Promise.

Chapter 8

Rome, Hercules, and the Mithraic Mysteries

Hercules' cousin Eurystheus ordered Hercules to clean King Augeas' stables. To make the job even more difficult, he said it had to be done in one day. King Augeas was a very wealthy man and had thousands of cattle—horses, cows, goats, and sheep. Hercules went to King Augeas and offered to clean his stables. "If I clean your stables in one day, will you give me a tenth of your cattle?" Hercules asked. King Augeas agreed, for he thought that it was an impossible task.

First, Hercules cut two holes in the wall where the stables were—one hole in each end. Then he dug two ditches to the stables from two nearby rivers. Next, he diverted the rivers to flow down the ditches to the stables. The water went in one hole and out the other, cleaning the stables in one day.

When Hercules went to King Augeus for his payment, the king angrily refused to pay him. They went before a judge, who ruled that King Augeus must pay Hercules.

Rome and Hercules

The city of Rome dates back to around 700 BC. Tribes of people called Italiis lived in southern Italy. One of the strongest of these was the Latins. The language of the Latin people became the language of Rome. To the north of the Latins, in an area called Etruria, lived a tribe called the Etruscans. The Etruscans had many trades and skills such as leatherworking, street paving, and weapons-making. For centuries there were struggles between the Latins and the Etruscans, but eventually they blended and became the world-dominating Romans.

Hercules, another figure found in the constellations, was a major god among the Romans. He is part of the house of Scorpio, as was Ophiuchus (Asclepius). On the planisphere we can find him above Ophiuchus. His is the figure of a mighty man, down on one knee, with his heel uplifted as if wounded. He has a great club in one hand and a three-headed monster in the other. His left foot is set directly on the head of Draco, the great dragon. One of the star names is "the branch," and another is "head of him who bruises." Long before the time of the Greeks and Romans, the Phoenicians worshipped this Hercules and honored him as being "a savior."[24] He represents the seed of the woman, come to bruise and destroy the serpent and anything belonging to the serpent's kingdom.

Hercules was the son of the god Zeus and the mortal Alcmene. His personal problems started at birth. The goddess Hera, sister-wife of Zeus, sent two witches to prevent his birth, but were tricked by Alcmene and sent to another room. Then Hera sent serpents to kill him in his cradle, but Hercules managed to strangle them both. He was brought up with the best tutors of the land and he had to learn to sing and play the lyre, but he would have much rather wrestled and fought to show his great strength. He became a successful hero, married, and had three strong sons. The goddess Hera could not tolerate this situation, so she sent a madness upon Hercules which put him into such a rage that he killed his own children. When he came to, he was overwhelmed with grief. His cousin Theseus convinced him to find a way to atone for his sins. He asked the oracle of Delphi what he needed to do. He was told he must be a slave of his cousin Eurystheus and perform ten labors for him. (Later, Eurystheus added two more labors.) These labors became known as the famous Twelve Labors of Hercules:

1. He killed the monstrous lion, whose hide was so tough it could not be pierced. He used one of the lion's teeth to remove his impenetrable hide, then wore the hide as protection.

2. He killed the many-headed Hydra. Hydra was the terrible monster which infested the Lernaean Lake. It was said to have a hundred heads and could not be killed simply by cutting off the heads. Unless the wound was burned with fire, two heads immediately grew out where there was only one before. Hercules succeeded in destroying this monster, helped by his faithful companion and charioteer Iiolaus. He applied a red-hot iron to the wound as head after head was severed. Hercules then dipped his arrows in the Hydra's blood for future use.

3. He captured the Erymanthian boar. This labor took him to the land of the centaurs. When the centaurs attacked him, he had to kill many of them; but he brought the boar back alive to Eurystheus. It was during this labor that he took part in the adventure of the hero Jason and the Argonauts, who searched for the Golden Fleece.

4. He rid the Stymphalian Lake of a swarm of dangerous birds, with feathers of brass, which were ravaging the countryside. He accomplished this feat by using a rattle given to him by Athena. The rattle startled the birds, and Hercules then shot them down with his arrows.

5. He pursued and caught a swift deer and carried it back alive. He spent over a year trying to catch this deer with the golden antlers. He finally brought it down with an arrow to its hoof.

6. As noted earlier, he cleaned the stables of King Augeas, which had held three thousand oxen for thirty years without ever being cleaned, by diverting two rivers so that they ran through the stables and cleaned them completely in a day. Eurystheus, however, argued that this labor should not count as one of Hercules' labors, because he had been paid.

7. He brought back the golden girdle of Hippolyta, queen of the Amazons. The Amazons were a group of fearless female warriors.

8. He brought back the four mares of King Diomedes, which had been trained to eat strangers.

9. He caught a fierce fire-breathing bull by seizing the charging bull by the horns.

10. He brought back a huge herd of red cows. Before he sailed off in a golden ship for this labor, Hercules pulled up two huge boulders and set them down on either side of the strait; to this day, they are called the Pillars of Hercules.

11. He was sent to bring back three golden apples from Hera's secret garden of the Hesperides, which were guarded by the dragon Ladon. On his way there, he passed the Titan Prometheus, who was chained on the Caucasus Mountains. Hercules took time to tear off Prometheus' chains; in gratitude, Prometheus warned Hercules not to pick the golden apples or he would die. He killed the dragon, and convinced Atlas who held up the earth and the heavens on his shoulders to get the apples for him while Hercules shouldered his burden. When he got back, Atlas did not want to take the weight back. Hercules said he would continue to hold up the earth and the heavens if Atlas would just take it for a moment so he could adjust his cloak so it would cushion his shoulders. When Atlas agreed and took the weight, Hercules picked up the apples and left.

12. Finally, Hercules was sent to the underworld to capture Cerberus, the three-headed watchdog of Hades and bring him back. Before he could enter the underworld, Hercules had to become initiated in the Eleusinian mysteries at the sacred city of Eleusis. He then journeyed to Hades where he had further adventures, including freeing his cousin Theseus from the chair of forgetfulness where he had been bound. He wrestled the dog Cerberus and brought him back to Eurystheus. Eurystheus

was so terrified that he told Hercules that all his labors were finished, and that he was to take Cerberus back to the underworld where he had found him.

Having performed these twelve labors, Hercules traveled all over Greece, performing great deeds and winning friends. He married Deianira and they lived happily for a time until he accidentally killed his father-in-law's cupbearer. It was an accident and he was forgiven by the king, but Hercules could not forgive himself and left the city with Deianira. When a centaur tried to rape Deianira, Hercules shot the centaur with one of the arrows Hercules had dipped in the blood of the Hydra. As the centaur was dying, he told Deianira that his blood possessed a special quality as a love potion and that she should take some of it in a vial. If she ever felt that Hercules was losing interest in her, she should sprinkle some on his shirt and he would be in love with her forever.

Again, Hercules and Deianira were happy for a time until Hercules helped Artemis kill a boar which was ravishing the kingdom, and was given Iole as a concubine. Hercules prepared a victory feast and sent word to Deianira to send him his best shirt to wear at the festival. Deianira, afraid that Hercules was now more fond of Iole than she, soaked his shirt in the blood of the centaur. As soon as Hercules put on the shirt, he was seized with agony. He did not die quickly but became weaker and weaker. He built a funeral pyre on Mount Etna, sacrificed himself, and went to live with the gods on Mount Olympus.

In Hercules, we see another "god-man." He goes against the roaring satanic lion and the heads of the great serpent. He slays the dragon and descends into hell to capture the triple-headed dog. He is wounded in one of his encounters and, still suffering, mounts the funeral pyre to die of his own accord. Many of these dramatic stories illustrate immortal truths. We find here some of the symbolism of the protoevangelium—the conqueror of the serpent who is bruised by the serpent.

Mystery Religions of Rome

The mystery religions included an initiation process whereby initiates would undergo hardships and experience sights and sounds both frightening and beautiful. They would be taught a variety of moral truths, along with each particular group's supposed insights into life and death.

The Mithraic mysteries, centered on the god Mithras, was found in the Roman Empire from the first century until the fourth century AD. The Iranian god Mithras may have inspired the religion, although the link between the Roman Mithraic mysteries and the religion of Persia (Iran) is debated.

Information about the Mithraic mysteries is found in underground temples called *mithraia*, of which many survive in and around Rome. Three scenes found in the wall of the *mithraia* have been written about extensively in attempts to understand the religion. The most prominent and well known is the so-called "tauroctomy" which shows Mithras killing a bull. This scene has no parallel with the Persian god Mithras. The other scenes found in the underground temples include a banquet scene which features Mithras and the sun god feasting on the slaughtered bull. The third common picture or iconography in the *mithraia* is that of Mithras being born from, or emerging from, a rock with a dagger in one hand and a torch in the other and wearing a Phrygian cap.

The origins of the Mithraic mysteries have been debated. One scholar, David Ulansey, writes about his theory that Mithras represents the god (and constellation) Perseus. On the planisphere, the constellation Perseus is shown above the bull Taurus. Perseus is holding in one hand a dagger and in the other the head of the Medusa, and he is looking away from the Medusa. The common myth about Perseus is that he is able to kill the Medusa because he avoids looking at her and thus is not turned to stone. Perseus is also shown sometimes wearing a Phrygian cap. It is curious that Mithras is holding a similar style dagger, wearing a Phrygian cap, and also looking away from his deed of killing the bull.[25]

Other scholars, such as Michael Speidel, associate Mithras with the sun god Orion. His thesis is that Mithras is more Hellenic than oriental (Persian). He writes that Mithras is the constellation Orion and that the myth of Mithras is largely the myth of the Greek hero Orion.[26]

Whether Mithras represents Orion or Perseus, they are both representing god-men who are "conquerors of the serpent," and as such come from ancient constellation symbols which are a prediction of Christ. In very ancient times, men copied onto the constellations the idea of Genesis 3:15, that of a woman-born conqueror of the evil one. This verse is a prediction of the coming of Christ. Down through the ages, men have attempted to understand this prediction and have spun fantastic tales to illustrate it.

Chapter 9

Persia, Balaam's Sacrifice, and the Magi

The weary travelers stopped to rest beside a well. The little town stretched out in front of them. The road marker said "Bethlehem." Had they finally arrived? Was this the place? They glanced into the well and then they saw it. The star! Reflected in the water at the bottom of the well was the bright star. They glanced up into the sky. There it was. The bright star was straight above Bethlehem.

The Great Civilization of Persia

One of the greatest civilizations of the ancient world was Persia. The heart of the Persian Empire was what is today modern Iran. The first true Persian Empire was ruled by the Achaemenid Dynasty. They called themselves Aryans but were known as

Persians since they came from the area called Pars. Before the Persian Empire, the area was controlled by the Medians; but Cyrus the Great (c. 550 BC) was able to overthrow the Median emperor (who happened to be his grandfather). This conquest was the beginning of the Persian Empire. Cyrus the Great conquered Media and much of the surrounding areas including Lydia and Neo-Babylon. He freed the Jews from their captivity in Babylon and allowed them to resettle Jerusalem. He worked with them to rebuild the city of Jerusalem and Solomon's temple, as told in the Old Testament. The empire lasted for more than two hundred years, until it was conquered by Alexander the Great.

At its peak the Persian Empire had an estimated population of fifty million people, which was at that time about half of the population of the known world. Ruling half the world gives the Persian Empire the claim to being one of the greatest empires of all time. Likewise, Cyrus the Great is viewed by history as one of the greatest rulers of all time. He seemed to take the interest of his people to heart. Although Cyrus conquered a very large area, he was not able to conquer Egypt. When he died, however, his son Cambyses was able to conquer Egypt; at that time Egypt became part of the Persian Empire.

Zarathustra

In establishing the Persian Empire, Cyrus the Great spread Zoroastrianism, a belief system based on the prophet Zarathustra. Zoroastrianism was a primary religion in the area of Persia until Mohammed brought Islam to the area.

It is not known when Zarathustra was born. Some historians place him as early as 1500 BC, and others as late as 700 BC. The religion he taught was monotheistic with the one god Ahura Mazda, who had no human form and could not be pictured. The faith Zarathustra taught is sometimes called a dualistic faith, with contrasts between light and dark and good and evil. Zarathustra taught that good thoughts lead to good words, and good words lead to good actions. In contrast, he taught that bad thoughts lead to bad words, which lead to bad actions. The sacred texts of Zoroastrianism are called the Avesta.

Animal Sacrifices

A curious passage in Numbers 22–24 of the Old Testament relates the story of Balaam, the Gentile, from the land of Pethor in northern Mesopotamia. When the Israelites camped in the plains of Moab, the Moabites were frightened and Balak the king of Moab sent for Balaam so he could curse the Israelites. Apparently Balaam enjoyed a considerable reputation as a successful prophet.

When the messengers came to Balaam, he told them to spend the night there, while Balaam sought the direction of the Lord. God told Balaam, "Do not go with them; you shall not curse the people, for they are blessed." In the morning Balaam told the messengers, "Go back to your land, for the LORD has refused to let me go with you" (Numbers 22:12–13).

Balak then sent additional messengers to persuade Balaam with a promise of great rewards. Balaam told the messengers, "Though Balak were to give me his house full of silver and gold, I could not do anything, either small or great, contrary to the command of the LORD my God." Balaam inquired of the Lord again and was told he could go "but only the word which I speak to you shall you do" (Numbers 22:18, 20).

When Balaam arrived, he and Balak went to the summit of the mountain where Balaam told Balak to "Build seven altars for me here and prepare seven bulls and seven rams for me here" (Numbers 23:1). Balak did as Balaam had said and offered a bull and a ram on each altar. We see here two non-Israelites, Balak and Balaam, offering animal sacrifices.

Animal sacrifices foreshadowed the ultimate sacrifice: that of Jesus Christ on the cross. Animal sacrifice has been a traditional part of religion since ancient times. We find animal sacrifices in every ancient culture. The central religious act in ancient Greece and Rome was the sacrifice of oxen, goats, and sheep. Sacrifice remains in the holy books of the world's major traditional religions, but most religions no longer practice sacrifice. Christians believe that the sacrifices in the Old Testament were a foreshadowing of Christ's sacrifice, and therefore are no longer necessary. The rending of the curtain in the temple when Christ died signified the end of animal sacrifices.

During the lifetime of Jesus, the temple in Jerusalem was the center of Jewish religious life. The temple was the place where animal sacrifices were carried out as the type of worship proscribed by the Law of Moses. The veil in the temple separated the Holy of Holies from the rest of the temple. The Holy of Holies was the place of God's presence which only the high priest could enter. He would only enter once a year into God's presence, to make atonement for the sins of all the people.

Since the temple was thirty to forty cubits high, the temple veil was about sixty feet high and was made of very thick fabric from blue, purple, and scarlet material and fine twisted linen. The size and thickness of this veil makes the event of its tearing momentous: "And Jesus cried out again with a loud voice and yielded up His spirit. And behold, the veil of the temple was torn in two from top to bottom; and the earth shook and the rocks were split" (Matthew 27:50–51).

The tearing of the veil at the moment of Christ's death showed that His sacrifice, His shedding of blood, was sufficient for the atonement of sin. Animal sacrifice was no longer needed. This symbolic event showed that Jesus Christ is the only way to God. Before Christ's death, the high priest had entered into God's presence through the veil.

Animal sacrifice points to Christ, the Redeemer. The universal practice of animal sacrifice shows us a parallel with the sacrifices performed by the first men mentioned in the Bible. When God found Adam and Eve hiding in the garden because of their shame for their nakedness, he clothed them in animal skins (Genesis 3:8–21). God sacrificed an animal to cover their naked bodies and their sin. Joseph Farah writes that this was the beginning of the sacrificial system.[27] The patriarchs Abel, Noah, Job, Abraham, Isaac, and Jacob all are recorded as performing animal sacrifices to God.

The historian George Stanley Faber discusses the parallels between the ancient pagan religions and the biblical stories of the patriarchs' worship. This worship included animal sacrifices, and also included similarities such as the places of worship, symbols, and moral codes. Faber points out, "The close resemblance of the whole Levitical [Jewish] ceremonial to the ceremonial among the Gentiles [pagans] has often been observed."[28] Their similarity arises from the fact that they both came from the patriarchal religion, the religion given by God to the first men. Although there are many differences in these acts of worship, there are also many similarities. It is these similarities which show their common origin.

Balaam's Prophecy

Let's return now to the story of Balak and Balaam. After they had offered their sacrifices, Balaam spoke his message. But he did not curse the Israelites as Balak had wanted him to do. Instead, he blessed them, which angered Balak greatly. Balaam prophesied of a coming deliverer/redeemer: "I see him, but not now; I behold him, but not near; a star shall come forth from Jacob, and a scepter shall rise from Israel, and shall crush through the forehead of Moab" (Numbers 24:17). Balaam's prophecy of the star was a prediction of the coming of the Redeemer (Christ).

Balaam may also have been a part of a group of scholars from Persia who studied the stars. The later magi, whom the Bible records as coming to Bethlehem to worship the new Messiah, were likely from Persia. They may have been familiar with Balaam's prophecy and with the prophecies of Daniel, who had been the most distinguished of the wise men (Daniel 6:3, 28) at the courts of Darius and of Cyrus the Persian. The magi saw the star in the east and apparently knew it signified the birth of "the King of the Jews," and they came to Jerusalem to find him. After consulting with Herod (and the chief priests and scribes), they went to Bethlehem to find the child. "[T]he star, which they had seen in the east . . . came and stood over the place where the Child was" (Matthew 2:9).

Some modern astronomers such as James Mullaney have suggested that the "star of Bethlehem" was likely a nova or supernova. A nova or supernova is the gigantic explosion of an existing but previously unknown star which then fades away after shining brightly for many months.[29] What a magnificent announcement a nova would have been.

An ancient legend says that when the magi came to Bethlehem, they saw the star's reflection in the water at the bottom of a well. That was how they knew the star was vertical over the village.

Ignatius, an apostolic father who lived closest to the time of the New Testament writers and died in 107, wrote the following about the star: "[It was] a star which so shone in heaven beyond all the stars, its newness caused excitement."[30] Eusebius, in the fourth century, made a study and came to this conclusion: "The star was new and a stranger among the usual lights of heaven, a strange star besides the usual ones, a strange and unusual star, not one of the many known stars, but being new and fresh."[31]

As noted, the three magi mentioned in the account of the birth of Jesus Christ are thought to have come from Persia. Zoroaster and the magi of Persia were skilled in astronomy; had identified the major planets, stars, and constellations; and were able to plot their movements with great accuracy. Zoroaster is reputed to have built an observatory to determine equinoxes and solstices. Is it possible that Zoroaster, in some way, knew about the coming Redeemer and his star and taught it to his disciples, the magi?

Chapter 10

China, the Astronomers, and the Altar of Heaven

Lu silently watched the great parade move by her home. Hidden in the bushes, she was careful not to be seen. She saw the men on horses. Both the men and the horses were highly decorated—the men with their bright uniforms, tall caps, and shining swords; and the horses draped with embroidered fabrics. Next came the elephants, lifting their trunks high in the air and stepping carefully beside their handlers. These huge animals carried highly decorated chairs, and seated in them were important-looking officials. Then came guards, ministers, and attendants, all dressed in the finest of attire. But no sounds came from the procession. It was a very solemn event.

Early China

The earliest civilizations in China grew up on the banks of the country's largest rivers, and the first towns appeared around the Huang He (Yellow River). The first dynasty marked the reign of the Xia, who ruled for four centuries around 2000 BC. Its founder, Yu, was credited with building dikes to control flooding and with making irrigation channels. The next dynasty (which lasted for more than six hundred years) was the Shang Dynasty, which was founded by Emperor Tang. His cities had many beautiful palaces and temples built of carved wood.

The Shang people grew millet, wheat, and rice, and kept cattle, pigs, sheep, dogs, and chickens. They hunted deer and wild pig. They used horses to draw plows, carriages, and chariots. They also raised mulberries in order to feed silkworms. A silkworm eats only mulberry leaves and spins a cocoon with silky threads; these threads are carefully unwound and used to make silk. For thousands of years the Chinese kept their secret of how to make silk, and as a result silk became so valuable that it was used in place of money for trade.

Legends say there was an empress named His-Ling Shi who lived at a very early time, even before the Shang dynasty. She planted mulberry groves to feed the silkworms, and learned how to make silk.

Chinese Astronomers

The Chinese have always observed and recorded major astronomical events. Around the time that the magi followed the star, there are two entries regarding an unusual astral event in the second year of Jian Ping of Emperor Xiao Ai. In the spring on the first month, a Bei comet was found at Altair.[32] The Chinese associated all phenomena associated with Altair as having to do with their border sacrifices.

The Chinese also recorded the astronomical event which the Bible tells us occurred as Jesus Christ hung on the cross. Before Jesus died, darkness fell over the whole land for three hours (Matthew 27:45). The Chinese historical documents record a highly significant solar eclipse which occurred around the time of Jesus' death, on the last day of the month, the day of Gui Hai. The emperor suspended all military activities and did not handle any official business for five days. He proclaimed, "My poor character has caused this calamity, that the sun and moon were veiled. I am fearful and trembling. What can I say?"[33]

Another entry referring to the same eclipse is also recorded: "Summer, fourth month [of the year], on the day of Ren Wu, the imperial edict read, 'Yin and Yang have mistakenly switched, and the sun and moon were eclipsed. The sins of all the people are now on one man. [The emperor] proclaims pardon to all under heaven.'"[34]

Perhaps the most incredible entry reads as follows: "Eclipse on the day of Gui Hai, Man from heaven died."[35] The Chinese appeared to have some understanding of the extraordinary significance of this eclipse.

The Border Sacrifice

There are parallels between the Chinese and the Jewish cultures. They have the honor of sharing the distinction for having the longest consecutively preserved cultures and histories in the world. The Chinese Christian author Chan Kei Thong writes that China's four millennia of history show an amazingly accurate knowledge of the one true God, whom the Jews called "Yahweh" (or Jehovah) and whom the Chinese reverently referred to as "Shang Di." Thong tells us that God left many markers scattered throughout Chinese history and culture pointing to Jesus Christ, the Son of God, who is therefore the fulfillment of the deepest longings of the Chinese people.[36]

The ancient rulers of China set up a godly way of ruling the people. Their book of Mencius teaches that when a ruler was no longer virtuous, the Mandate of Heaven—the God-given right to rule—was withdrawn. Such a ruler should be removed. Mencius also wrote that filial piety (respect for fathers) is the cornerstone of good society.[37]

Another similarity between the Chinese and Jewish cultures is the importance of sacrifice in the practice of their religion. The emperor was expected to sacrifice at the Altar of Heaven three times a year. Of course, not every emperor was faithful. The most important of these sacrifices was the border sacrifice, so called because it usually took place on the southern outskirts (border) of the imperial city. It was offered at the winter solstice, the shortest day of the year (December 21 or 22). The common English name "Temple of Heaven" is actually a misnomer; the Chinese name (Tian Tan) should be translated "Altar of Heaven." According to records at the altar complex, twenty-two emperors made 654 sacrifices to Shang Di at the Altar of Heaven over a period of about five hundred years. Hundreds of tourists now visit the Altar of Heaven complex daily.

The current Altar of Heaven complex was built in 1421, but China's historical records show that sacrifices were performed by many ancient rulers and continued until the collapse of the last dynasty in 1911. We will show the beautiful and elaborate ceremony using the Ming Dynasty version of the ceremony, as recorded in The Collected Statutes of the Ming Dynasty and as explained by Chan Kei Thong in his book, *Finding God in Ancient China.*[38]

Preparation for the Ceremony

Three months before the day of Sacrifice

Officials went to select unblemished sacrificial animals, usually calves. We also find that in the biblical sacrifices, an unblemished animal was required.

Six days before the Sacrifice

The emperor and many officers went to the altar mound and made a proclamation of the coming sacrifice.

Five days before the Sacrifice

A prince went to inspect the sacrificial animals.

Three days before the Sacrifice

The emperor began a fast and was required to abstain from drinking wine and eating meat. He was also to shun the company of women and was not to enjoy any kind of entertainment. He did not handle any criminal cases, in order to keep his mind pure. During this time, he wrote prayers on wooden boards, which would later be read in the ceremony. Government officials joined him in this three-day fast at their own residences.

We see a similarity with the Jewish observances; in the preparation for the Jewish Day of Atonement, a commanded fast was to be observed.

Two days before the Sacrifice

The emperor inspected the written prayers, the jade offerings, and incense at the Hall of Great Harmony within the Forbidden City.

One day before the Sacrifice

The emperor left the Forbidden City by the Meridian Gate with an impressive and colorful entourage of more than five thousand soldiers, elephants, horses, guards, ministers, eunuchs, and attendants all dressed in finest attire. The procession was a solemn event. No women, not even the empress, were permitted to participate. Absolute silence was maintained along the entire three-mile route to the Altar of Heaven.

The entourage entered by the West Gate. The emperor went immediately to the Imperial Vault and prostrated himself before a tablet inscribed with Name above All Names (Huang Tian Shang Di), meaning Supreme Lord of the Great Heaven. China's emperor, the most powerful man in the most powerful nation of the world at that time, humbled himself with his face to the floor before Shang Di. He knelt three times and kowtowed three times, with each kneeling for a total of nine kowtows (prostrations).

The Day of Sacrifice

The day of sacrifice began seven quarter hours before sunrise. Since the sun rises at 6 am at the winter solstice, the ceremony would have begun at 4:15. The emperor wore robes of plum-colored silk, a black satin cap, and blue satin boots; and he was carried in a ceremonial sedan chair. The bell of the Hall of Abstinence rang continuously.

At the south gate of the inner hall, the emperor changed into sacrificial robes used only for the ceremony. He washed his face and hands in a golden basin and proceeded to the altar mound. Again, there is a similarity to the Jewish ceremonial law here. In the tabernacle was a bronze laver, and the priests were to wash their hands and feet before beginning any priestly service such as the sacrifices.

The ceremony consisted of nine stages.

Stage 1: Welcoming Di

The emperor was led to the second-tier platform on the south side of the Mound, where he stood before a yellow canopy facing the shrine for Huang Tian Shang Di. The bell stopped ringing. Branches of pine and cypress were burnt. Nine incense handlers gave out fresh incense of cedar, sandalwood, and pine. Fragrant smoke rose. Musicians began playing the music and singers started to sing the "Zhong He":

> Of old in the beginning, there was the great chaos, without form and dark. The five planets had not begun to revolve, nor the two lights to shine. In the midst of it there existed neither form nor sound. You, O spiritual Sovereign, came forth in Your sovereignty, and first did separate the impure from the pure. You made heaven; You made earth; You made man. All things became alive with reproducing power.

This song has many similarities to the words of Genesis 1:1–2, which tells us, "In the beginning God created the heavens and the earth. The earth was formless and void."

Next, the emperor was guided to a position in front of the shrine on the highest-tier platform. He again performed the "three kneelings and the nine kowtows." The second sacred song "Yuan He" was sung:

Lord Di, when You separated the Yin and the Yang [i.e. the heavens and the earth], Your creative work had begun. You did produce, O Spirit, the seven elements [i.e. the sun and the moon and the five planets]. Their beautiful and brilliant lights lit up the circular sky and square earth. All things were good. I [Chen], Your servant, thank You fearfully, and, while I worship, present this memorial to You, O Di, calling You Sovereign.

This song has many similarities to the words of Genesis 1:16–18: "And God made the two great lights, the greater light to govern the day, and the lesser light to govern the night; He made the stars also . . . and God saw that it was good."

Stage 2: Offering of Gems and Silk

Those in charge of the jade and silks approached the altar, each carrying a basket. The third song was played:

You have promised, O Di, to hear us, for You are our Father. I, Your child, dull and unenlightened, am unable to show forth my dutiful feelings. I thank You, that You have accepted our pronouncement. Honorable is Your great name. With reverence we spread out these gems and silks, and, as swallows rejoicing in the spring, praise your abundant love.

In the Old Testament, God is frequently referred to as "Father." In 2 Samuel 7:14, the prophet Nathan is given these words from God, referring to David: "I will be a father to him and he will be a son to Me."

The silks were covered with prayers that were written on them. These prayers were read before Shang Di, and then the silk was taken to be burned in the furnace.

Stage 3: Offering of the Zu

The Zu was a large wooden platter which held the sacrificial meat of a roasted calf. This was brought to the emperor along with a thick, fragrant, hot broth which was poured over the meat. The emperor presented the broth and the Zu before the shrine of Shang Di and also before his ancestors. He knelt before Shang Di and then knelt once in front of two groups of ancestors, presenting the broth and then did the same with the Zu. The musicians played "Yu He":

> The great feast has been set forth, and the sound of celebration is like thunder. The Sovereign Spirit promises to enjoy our offering, and Your servant's heart feels like a particle of dust. The meat has been boiled in the large caldrons, and the fragrant provisions have been prepared. Enjoy the offering, O Di, then shall all the people be blessed. I [Chen], Your servant, am filled with thanksgiving. How blessed I am!

Stage 4: First Presentation of Wine—Martial Dance

At this point, dancers with shields and hatchets came from the south gate to perform the Wu, a martial dance. The dance was accompanied by music as the singers sang "Shou He":

> The great and lofty One pours out His grace and love; how unworthy are we to receive it. I, His foolish

servant, while I worship, hold this precious cup, and praise Him, whose years have no end.

The Old Testament prophet Isaiah also tells of the high and lofty God who is eternal: "For thus says the high and exalted One who lives forever, whose name is Holy" (Isaiah 57:15).

The wine official presented the ceremonial wine to the emperor, while he was kneeling. The emperor went to the prayer table and prostrated himself three times. A prayer was read, which the emperor himself had written during his three-day fast. Here is part of the prayer of Emperor Jia Jing, who reigned from 1522–1566:

> O awesome Creator, I look up to You. How imperial is the expansive heavens. Now is the time when the masculine energies of nature begin to be displayed, and with the great ceremonies I reverently honor You. Your servant, I am but a reed or willow; my heart is but as that of an ant; yet have I received Your favoring Mandate, appointing me to the government of the empire. I deeply cherish a sense of my ignorance and foolishness, and am afraid lest I prove unworthy of Your abundant grace. Therefore will I observe all the rules and statutes, striving, insignificant as I am, to be faithful. Far distant here, I look up to Your heavenly palace. Come in Your precious chariot to the altar. Your servant, I bow my head to the earth reverently expecting Your abundant grace. All my officers are here arranged along with me, dancing and worshipping before You. All

the spirits accompany You as guards, from the east to the west. Your servant, I prostrate myself to meet You, and reverently look up for Your coming, O Di. O that You would promise to accept our offerings, and regard us, while we worship You because Your goodness is inexhaustible!

Stage 5: Second Presentation of Wine—Civil Dance
This was similar to the first presentation in Stage 4. The song "Tai He" was performed:

> All the numerous species of living things are indebted to Your grace for their beginning. Men and things are all enveloped in Your benevolence, O Di. All living things are indebted to Your goodness, but who knows from Whom his blessings come to him. It is You alone, O Lord who are the true Ancestor of billions and trillions of things.

Stage 6: Final Presentation of Wine
The emperor approached Shang Di with his final toast, as the musicians and singers performed "Yong He":

> The precious feast is wide displayed; the gem-filled benches are arranged; the pearly wine is presented, with music and dances. The spirit of harmony is present; men and beasts are happy. The breast of His servant is troubled, that he is unable to repay his debts.

Stage 7: Removal of the Offerings

The offerings were removed and the song "Xian He" was performed:

> The service of song is completed, but our poor sincerity cannot be expressed. Your sovereign goodness is infinite. As a potter, You have made all living things. Great and small are sheltered [by Your love]. Imprinted on the heart of Your poor servant is the sense of Your goodness, so that my feeling cannot be fully displayed. With great kindness You do bear with us, and, notwithstanding our demerits, do grant us life and prosperity.

This analogy of God as the Potter is used many times in the Bible, perhaps the most famous being found in Isaiah 64:8: "But now, O Lord, You are our Father, we are the clay, and You our potter; and all of us are the work of Your hand."

Stage 8: Sending Off Di

A magnificent round ceremonial ashen jade, a symbol of heaven, was removed from the shrine and later carried back to the Treasure House. The song "Qing He" was performed:

> With reverent ceremonies the record has been presented, and You, O sovereign Spirit, have accepted our service. The dances have all been performed, and nine times the music has responded. Grant, O Di, Your great blessing to increase the happiness of my house. The instruments of metal and precious stones have given out their melody. The jeweled girdles of the officers have emitted their tinkling sound. Spirits and

men rejoice together, praising Di, the Lord. While we celebrate His great name, what limit can there be, or what measure? Forever He sets fast the high heavens, and establishes the solid earth. His government is everlasting. His unworthy servant, I bow my head; I lay it in the dust, bathed in His grace and glory.

During this song, the emperor and all the officials made a final prostration, kneeling three times and kowtowing nine times.

Stage 9: The Burnt Offering

The officials took the bull, the written prayer scroll, the silks, the incense, and other offerings and placed them into the roaring flames of the furnaces located at the sides of the altar mound. The emperor stood on the top tier facing east to watch the burnt offering. The sun rose in the distance and the musicians played "Xi He":

We have worshipped and written the Great Name on this gem-like sheet. Now we display it before Di, and place it in the fire. These valuable offerings of silks and fine meats we burn also, with these sincere prayers, that they may ascend in volumes of flames up to the distant sky. All the ends of the earth look up to Him. All human beings on the earth, rejoice together in the Great Name.[39]

In this chapter we see many parallels between the Chinese border sacrifices and the Old Testament sacrifices. Animal sacrifices were a foreshadowing of Christ's sacrifice, which was the fulfillment of the Sacred Promise.

Chapter 11

The Norse People and the Myth of Thor

George silently rowed his little boat to the lookout island. The sun was just setting in the western sky, leaving beautiful streaks of red. "Red sky at night, sailor's delight," he thought to himself. At fourteen years of age, he felt very important to be able to do the night watch. He pulled the boat to shore and climbed the lookout tower. No, he would never fall asleep, he told himself. For hours he scanned the sea, and then, he saw them! Waves marked their movement. It looked like hundreds of them. He pushed down the terror rising within him so he could act. He practically jumped off the tower, climbed into his boat, and rowed as fast as he had ever rowed to the first house, where the runners and the men on horses were dispatched.

The Norse People

"Viking" and "Norse" are two words that can be used inter-changeably. They refer to the Indo-European people who lived in Scandinavia during the Viking Age. The different names may refer somewhat to their different lifestyles. The Norse were traders, whereas the Vikings were primarily farmers who were sometimes pirates and warriors who traveled in their longboats to faraway parts of the world, to trade and sometimes to conquer other lands in order to expand their territory and to settle.

The Viking raiders were made up of landowners, freemen, and any adventuresome young clan members who were looking for booty overseas. At home they were farmers, but at sea they were raiders and pillagers. They raided and colonized wide areas of Europe from the seventh to eleventh centuries. Their burning, plundering, and killing earned them the name "Viking," which means "pirate" in the early Scandinavian languages.

Most of what is known about the origin of the Norse and Viking people is derived from the evidence of language. The Germanic languages include English, Norweigian, Swedish, Danish, Dutch, and German. Various Germanic tribes migrated into Italy, Gaul, Spain, and North Africa. Many merged with other people groups such as the Danes in Denmark, the Swedes in Sweden, and the Saxons in England.

Tacitus was a senator and a historian of the Roman Empire. He wrote and published a book now known as the *Germania* in 98 AD. He told that the Germans were sheep and cattle farmers and that most of their food came from milk, cheese, and meat, but that they also grew grain, root crops, and vegetables. According to most historians, the fall of the Roman Empire in 476 AD resulted from the successful attempt of the Germanic people to occupy the lands of the Roman Empire.

The eastern Germanic people remained migratory for a longer period of time, whereas the western Germanic people were more settled, with an agricultural base which allowed them to support more people. They periodically cleared forest land to extend their agriculture. The Germanic people created a strong military and were fierce in battle. Their love of battle appeared to be linked with their religion; two of their most important gods, Odin (also called Woden) and his son Thor were gods of war. The leaders of the clans were called chieftains, and one of their responsibilities was to keep the warriors united.

The Vikings terrorized Europe between 700 AD and 1100 AD. The Viking navigators used the sun and stars to guide them. They also relied on landmarks such as islands. When they invaded a new territory, they usually came with a few hundred ships and thousands of warriors. They were known for their surprise attacks. They could row their light boats into shallow rivers. They fought with axes and used both hands to swing their axes at enemies.

The Vikings' skills in sailing and shipmaking gave them the ability to travel farther and faster than most sailors of their time. Their fast, low-draft longship had an average length of one hundred feet with a width of twenty-five feet, could carry two hundred armed men with fifty oars, and could sometimes achieve speeds of eleven knots (more than twelve miles per hour).

When the areas they had conquered converted to Christianity, the Old Norse values were weakened. Many of the Norse and Vikings eventually became part of the cultures they had come in contact with. The Danish Vikings who invaded England became part of the English culture, while those who settled Normandy became French.

Earliest History

The Genesis writer identifies where the sixteen grandsons of Noah repopulated after the flood. It is easy to find these sixteen places because people in various areas often called themselves by the name of their common ancestor and also sometimes named their land, major rivers, and major cities by his name. In addition, they sometimes claimed their ancestor as their god. All sixteen grandsons can be traced to Europe, Asia, and Africa.

Two of the grandsons, Gomer and Tiras, both sons of Japheth, can be traced to the Germans and to the Vikings. The Bible says Gomer settled in the "north quarters." The Gauls in the first century were called Gomerites, and the Welsh language itself has been called Gomeraeg. One of the sons of Gomer was Ashkenaz, which is the Hebrew word for Germany.

Josephus wrote that Tiras, another grandson of Noah, became the ancestor of the Thirsians (Thracians). Tiras was worshipped by his descendants as Thuras (Thor), the god of thunder.

The basic dress of the Thracian and Viking warriors was a tunic, a cloak or cape, a cap, and boots. The cloak or cape was thrown over one shoulder. They carried a shield and spear, plus a small sword or dagger.

Thor

Thor, the son of Odin, was the god of thunder and of the sky in Norse and old Germanic mythology. The thunder god is known for his chief weapon, the mighty hammer Mjellnir or Crusher, which returned magically to his hand like a boomerang when he threw it. His hammer caused lightning which flashed across the sky when he used it. Thor also wore a magical belt that doubled his strength, and he owned a pair of goats that pulled his chariot across the sky.

Hymir was the father of the god Tyr. Hymir owned a large kettle, and Tyr and Thor paid Hymir a visit to get this kettle. During that visit Thor and Hymir went fishing, using an ox for bait. Something bit the ox, and when Thor drew up his line he realized that he had hooked Jormungand, the giant serpent. Putting his feet on the ocean floor, Thor pulled and pulled on the line while the serpent spit out poison. Just as Thor was about to strike the serpent with his hammer, Hymir cut the line and the serpent sank back down. The myths say they will fight again on the day called Ragnarok, the end of the world. At that day, Thor will kill the serpent but will die from its poison.[40]

Again, we see in this myth a type of the battle described in Genesis 3:15. Thor struggles with the serpent and will eventually kill it, even though he will die from its poison. In Genesis the man born of a woman conquers the serpent, even though he is bruised by this serpent. The thread of the Redeemer continues to appear throughout the globe.

Chapter 12

Aztecs and the God Quetzalcoatl

Picture a feathered serpent, perhaps looking like a flying dragon. One account describes the god Quetzalcoatl as crimson-breasted, with iridescent, emerald feathers that shimmered in the sunlight, looking golden-green to blue-violet.[41] Now imagine a creature like this flying. As its wings beat the air, sunlight would cause its feathers to sparkle with iridescent colors—perhaps the colors of the rainbow. It might look like flying fire, certainly something that could awe any observer.

There are many reports from the middle ages of flying serpents in many parts of the world. One report comes from Penllyne, Wales, as described by Marie Trevelyan: The winged serpents were beautiful and "looked as though they were covered with jewels of all sorts. Some of them had crests sparkling with all the colours of the rainbow." When they were disturbed, they glided swiftly through the air "sparkling all over" to their hiding places.[42]

Some commentators have suggested the fiery flying serpent may have been similar to pterosaurs. Pterosaurs were reptiles, close cousins of dinosaurs. Some large forms are called Quetzalcoatlus. When it was named in 1975, scientists estimated the largest Quetzalcoatlus fossils had a wingspan of up to forty feet.

The Aztec Civilization

The Aztecs likely originated as nomadic tribes from northern Mexico who arrived in Middle America around the beginning of the thirteenth century. They established the magnificent capital city of Tenochtitlan and became the dominant force in central Mexico, bringing many of the region's city-states under their control.

The Aztec warriors swept aside their rivals. They wore padded cotton armor and carried a wooden shield covered in hide. Their weapons included clublike swords, spears, and bows and arrows. Some of the warriors wore spectacular feather and animal-skin costumes and headdresses to show their rank.

The Aztecs drained swampy land to make it into fertile land for farming. Their sophisticated system of cultivation and irrigation enabled them to feed their large population. Typical crops were maize (corn), beans, squash, potatoes, tomatoes, and avocados. Bustling markets were visited by as many as fifty thousand people on major market days. They also fished and hunted rabbits, armadillos, snakes, coyotes, and wild turkey.

The Aztec civilization was highly structured, with a strict caste system. At the top were nobles, and at the bottom were serfs and slaves. In the great cities of the Aztec Empire, magnificent temples and statues showed the people's devotion to the many Aztec gods, including Quetzalcoatl, the "Feathered Serpent."

When the Spanish invaded Tenochtitlan, they were impressed by the city's splendor and magnificent structures such as the Templo Mayor pyramid. A huge sacred precinct with temples and a monumental ball court dominated the city. Large canals crisscrossed the city and were surrounded by raised and flooded fields. There were also dikes, fresh-water reservoirs, and beautiful flower gardens scattered around the city. The entire city was designed to awe an observer. It inspired terror in visiting nobles, who could see the Aztecs wealth and power.

The Aztec empire came to an abrupt end when it was conquered by Spanish explorers in 1519. The ninth emperor, Montezuma II, was taken prisoner by Hernán Cortes and died in captivity. Montezuma's successors were unable to defeat Cortes and his forces. With the capture of Tenochtitlan in 1521, the Aztec Empire came to an end.

It is possible that the Spanish conquerors led by Cortez may have been helped by a myth of the Aztecs. The Aztecs believed that the god Quetzalcoatl would return some day, and thought the Spanish conqueror to be that god. The Spanish conquerors brought the disease smallpox to the Aztecs, and that disease may have been more fatal to the Aztecs than the force of Spanish arms. Montezuma's successor himself succumbed to smallpox after ruling for only a few weeks.

Quetzalcoatl

The earliest known representations of the feathered serpent covered the sides of the large pyramid at Teotihuacan, in central Mexico. This structure is known as the Temple of

Quetzalcoatl, or the Feathered Serpent Pyramid, and dates from 150 to 200 AD.

The god worshipped by the Aztecs as Quetzalcoatl may have originated as a ruler of the Toltecs named Topiltzin Quetzalcoatl, whom tradition pictures as a reformer. It was said that "under his benevolent rule no human sacrifice was permitted, only that of animals."[43] One story says that a rival of his tricked him and forced him into exile. According to a long-held tradition, he would one day return and reclaim his throne. The legends of Topiltzin became so important that rulers would sometimes claim direct descent from Topiltzin Quetzalcoatl in order to legitimize their reign.

Quetzalcoatl, the Aztec god of wind and learning, was one of several important gods in the Aztec pantheon. "Coatl" means serpent and "Quetzal" means feathers, and he is sometimes pictured as a feathered serpent (much like a dragon). Sometimes he is also pictured as a man with a beard. Sometimes he is pictured as the wind god, with a mask with two pipes, through which the wind blew. According to the myths, Quetzalcoatl was born to a virgin named Chimalman, to whom the god Ontevl appeared in a dream. In another version of the myth, the virgin Chimalman became pregnant with Quetzalcoatl by swallowing an emerald.

Quetzalcoatl was known as an inventor of writing and of the calendar. He taught the people how to plant corn and was sometimes seen as a symbol of death and resurrection. Sometimes the honored gods of the pagans are said to have taught the people many good things; Quetzalcoatl taught the people how to plant corn, writing, and the use of the calendar. In chapter 4, we saw that Osiris was viewed as a primeval king of Egypt who taught the people how to plant crops and who gave them laws and religious instruction. In ancient history it appears that sometimes honored ancestors, after their death, were worshipped as gods.

It was said that Quetzalcoatl was coerced into becoming drunk and cavorted with his sister. The next morning he felt shame and remorse and had his servants build him a stone chest. Then, lying in the chest, he set himself on fire. His ashes rose into the sky and his heart followed.[44]

In the story of Quetzalcoatl we find some elements typical of the myths from other areas of the world, such as the fact that he sacrifices himself similar to the way Hercules did. This "dying and rising god" may be another example flowing from the knowledge men had in the beginning of the coming of the Redeemer.

Flying Serpents

Since the story of the fall of Adam, the serpent has become a symbol of Satan or evil, but not always. The word "Seraph" or "Saraph" signifies a flying serpent (dragon). The flying serpent was an animal of great beauty, with scales or feathers of gold, which could look like fire as the rays of the sun struck it while it rapidly flew through the air. The flying serpent was often included with other symbols relating to the cherubic symbols. The Rabbi Bechai observes that "this is the mystery of our holy language, that a serpent is called 'Seraph' as an angel is called 'Seraph.'"[45] The flying serpent is often found among pagan symbols.

The fiery serpent is mentioned in the Bible in Numbers 21:6. In this account, the Lord sent fiery serpents among the people because of their complaining. Moses put a brazen serpent on a pole, and when those who were bitten looked on the brazen serpent they did not die. In Isaiah 30:6 the beasts of the Negev, the Palestine desert, are referred to as "the lioness and lion, viper and flying serpent." The Hebrew word here for serpent is *seraph*. The Greek historian Herodotus, who lived in the fifth century BC, wrote of flying serpents that inhabited the Arabian desert and sometimes attacked Egypt.[46]

Samuel Bochart, a writer of the seventeenth century, described an ancient Hebrew work *Porta Coeli* mentioning how "the flying seraph sets fire to the air, corrupting [poisoning] all that is near it."[47]

In John 3:14–16, Jesus told his followers, "And as Moses lifted up the serpent in the wilderness, even so must the Son of Man be lifted up; so that whoever believes will in Him have eternal life. For God so loved the world, that He gave His only begotten Son, that whoever believes in Him shall not perish, but have eternal life."

There is something about feathered serpents and flying dragons that touches the imagination of us all. It is easy to recognize the awe that could be inspired by these creatures. But in worshipping these creatures as gods, the Aztecs also assigned to them some of the features we find in the myths of Greece and Scandinavia—that of a god born to a human mother, a god who sacrifices himself. And so we see bits of truth flowing down through history—a knowledge of the coming of a Redeemer to save mankind.

Chapter 13

The Resurrection of Jesus Christ and the Shroud of Turin

Henry pressed his nose against the windowpane and watched the long line of people filing past his house. Some looked like they had come a long distance; they were leaning on their walking sticks and wiping perspiration from their foreheads.

"Mama, where are all those people going?" Henry asked.

"They are going to the church to view the holy shroud."

"Can we go?" Henry begged.

"As soon as your father comes home, we will join the crowd."

Later, Henry and his brother and his mother and father joined the crowd on the road near their home. As they approached the church, Henry saw a large white cloth hanging from the balcony in front of the church. As he drew closer he could see the faint outline of a man. Everyone marveled that 1,500 years after his death, they were witnessing something which had touched the body of Jesus Christ.

"How did the marks get there?" Henry asked his mother.

"We don't know," she replied.

The Death of Resurrection of Jesus Christ

Two thousand years ago the death and resurrection of Jesus Christ shook the earth, literally and figuratively. The Bible records that when Jesus died on the cross, the earth shook and darkness covered the sky: "And Jesus cried out again with a loud voice, and yielded up His spirit. And behold, the veil in the temple was torn in two from top to bottom; and the earth shook and the rocks were split. . . . [The centurion and his fellow guards] became very frightened and said, 'Truly this was the Son of God!'" (Matthew 27:50–51, 54).

This event shook the world in more ways than one. Men and women down through the ages have put their hope in Jesus Christ. Jesus told his followers that if they believed in him, they too could look forward to a resurrected body when they died.

The Shroud of Turin is a fourteen-foot-long and three-foot-wide linen cloth believed to have been draped vertically over the body of Christ after his death. A faint outline of his body appears on the cloth, along with many blood marks. The Gospels mention the burial cloth being purchased by Joseph of Arimathea and seen by Peter in the empty tomb (Matthew 27:59; John 20:5–7).

The Shroud of Turin has been revered by Christians for many centuries. It has, in the past century, arguably received more scientific scrutiny than any other relic on Earth. Many books have been written about it, and many professional peer-reviewed papers have been written. We will now take a look at just a few of those books.

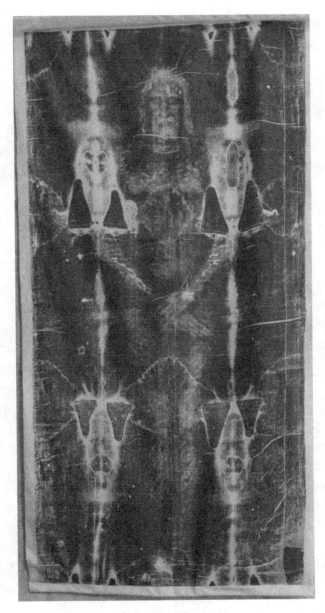

Shroud of Turin

A Doctor at Calvary by Dr. Pierre Barbet

Dr. Pierre Barbet's book, *A Doctor at Calvary* was published in France in 1950.[48] Dr. Barbet was a French specialist in archeology and scriptural studies as well as a medical doctor. In 1932 and 1935 he did anatomical studies, after witnessing the exposition of the shroud in 1931. He began his research in order to determine whether the shroud's markings corresponded with the realities of anatomy and physiology. He began with an open mind, equally ready to affirm that the shroud was a fraud or to recognize its authenticity. He was gradually forced to agree that, on every single point, its markings were exact and authentic.

Dr. Barbet pointed out that the Gospels merely state that Jesus was scourged and crucified. People reading the Gospels shortly after they were written would have known the intense suffering caused by scourging and crucifixion, but today we most likely do not realize its extent. The shroud shows that there are more than one hundred scourge marks on the body, from the beating received using the Roman flagrum, a whip which had two balls of lead or a small bone near the end of the whip. This whip would rip the skin during the beating. Most of the marks are on the back, but some are on the chest. Carrying the cross would have further bruised an already excoriated skin on his shoulders and back. The crown of thorns that was placed on him was like a cap, covering his head completely. On the back of the man in the shroud, one can see flows of blood covering the head.

One of the more sobering of the blood marks is the appearance of two streams of blood running down the figure's arms about ten degrees apart. These marks are an indication of crucifixion, since when a person hung on a cross the only way he could breathe was to push himself up by his feet for a short time in order to exhale. Then the weight of his body would pull him back down. This action creates two lines of blood flow on his arms. Although the arms are nailed while extended outward, they would become more vertical when the cross was put in place as they would hold the weight of the body.

Pictures and paintings of the crucifixion often show the nails through Jesus' palms. However, the shroud shows that the nails went through the wrists. This detail needs to be the accurate representation, as the palms could not hold the weight of the body. When a nail is placed through the wrist, it damages a nerve causing the thumb to turn inward. On the shroud the thumbs are not visible, indicating that they must have been retracted inward.

Report on the Shroud of Turin by Dr. John H. Heller

This book tells the story of forty American scientists who went to Turin in 1978 and spent a week making an intensive study of the shroud, using modern equipment.[49] This team represented the Shroud of Turin Research Project (STURP). Their tests led them to conclude that the image in every way conforms to that of a man who had been crucified in the Roman manner, and that the blood stains are indeed human blood. They were convinced that the shroud was not a forgery. The results of the STURP research were published in twenty peer-reviewed scientific journal articles in the four years following the team's work in Turin.

After the research by the STURP team, there was renewed interest in the shroud. Newspaper and magazine articles were written, and a TV documentary was produced. Then in 1988 a carbon-14 testing was done on the shroud, which showed it to be of medieval age; as a result, interest in the shroud waned.

However, many people felt that the carbon-14 testing was in error, and research and interest continued. The Turin Shroud Center of Colorado was begun by some STURP members, and several conferences on the Shroud of Turin have been held, at which researchers discussed recent discoveries and theories.

The Shroud: Fresh Light on the 2,000-Year-Old Mystery by Ian Wilson

Ian Wilson had a fifty-year fascination with the Shroud of Turin after beginning serious research in 1966. His prime focus has been the shroud's history.[50]

He begins his book with a story of a tour in Turkey, undertaken with Mark Guscin, to find information regarding the shroud's early years. Many Christian churches and artifacts have been destroyed by the Muslims, so archeological research can be difficult for Christians. They did find a mosaic of the "Image of Edessa" in Sanliurfa (the modern name for the ancient town of Edessa).

Wilson's book reads like a mystery novel, as he finds and locates ancient artifacts and icons. The image of Edessa is believed to be the same cloth now known as the Shroud of Turin. This cloth arrived in Constantinople in 944 and then disappeared from there in 1204 when the city was looted during the fourth Crusade. In 1350 it arrived in Europe and was exhibited in Lirey, France. The mystery of the cloth's whereabouts during the first nine hundred years is researched by Wilson, as well as its disappearance for 150 years after the looting of Constantinople. Reading old letters and writings by Christian leaders during that time gives him some clues.

Wilson includes pictures in his book of old sixth- and seventh-century icons of Christ. He tells how one amazing clue led to linking together the Image of Edessa with the Shroud of Turin. It was noticed that one of the seventh-century icons of Christ had on the forehead between the eyebrows a topless square which did not make much artistic sense. In looking at the Shroud of Turin they found the same feature, probably just a flaw in the weave. They wondered if the seventh-century artists were looking at the shroud while painting their icons (pictures) of Christ.

French scholar Paul Vignon found an additional fourteen similarities occurring on numerous Byzantine Christ portraits which seemed to derive from features visible on the face of the man in the Shroud of Turin, such as two strands of hair in the forehead, a transverse streak across the forehead, a raised right eyebrow, heavily accentuated "owlish" eyes, enlarged left nostril, and hairless area between the lower lip and beard.

Wilson's book gives much detail on how the Image of Edessa came to be viewed as the same cloth as the Shroud of Turin, thereby identifying the shroud's whereabouts during its first nine hundred years.

Test the Shroud: At the Atomic and Molecular Levels by Mark Antonacci[51]

Mark Antonacci has followed the research and discoveries found concerning the Shroud of Turin. He pulls together the current knowledge and history related to the shroud. In addition to the medical understanding of the blood marks and the scientific searches for an understanding of how the faint outline of the man in the shroud came to be, he points out some of the other evidence embedded in the shroud.

It is possible that, with great magnification, some features of a Pontius Pilate coin can be seen over the eyes. Coins were sometimes used at Jewish burials to close the eyes. A limestone sample taken from the foot region of the man in the shroud is a close match to the same rock shelf of the Holy Sepulcher and Garden Tomb in Jerusalem. Pollen grains identified on the shroud match species of flowers found in Jerusalem.

Antonacci shows some of the more recent theories regarding how the image may have been formed. Some scientists have suggested that some type of radiation may have occurred when Christ was resurrected, creating the image and moving the blood marks to the cloth without disturbing their edges. He also shows how a radiation event could cause an incorrect carbon-14 dating.

The Turin Shroud Center of Colorado

John Jackson, who has earned a PhD in physics, is president of the Turin Shroud Center of Colorado. It was he who led the large research team to study the shroud in 1978, as told above in *Report on the Shroud* by Dr. John H. Heller. Since then, research has continued.

In 2017 the Turin Shroud Center of Colorado and John Jackson published *The Shroud of Turin: A Critical Summary of Observations, Data, and Hypotheses*. In this work, the center's scholars provide an up-to-date summary of what is known about the shroud, drawing on TSC's tens of thousands of hours of shroud research. They present the evidence and the ongoing theories, and evaluate the theories in a scientific manner. Dr. Jackson and his associates hold the position that the Shroud of Turin is in fact the burial shroud of Jesus of Nazareth.[52]

At the St. Louis International Shroud Conference, held in October of 2014, one of the presenters from the Turin Shroud Center asked for a show of hands of those who had come to the reasoned judgment, based on dedicated study, that the shroud is the same cloth that wrapped the body of Jesus of Nazareth. About two-thirds of the 160 assembled participants raised their hands. A second question followed: Had the judgment of "authentic" changed their lives? Roughly the same number of hands were raised.

Why Is the Resurrection Important to Us?

In all civilizations, a golden age is remembered and recorded when life was perfect. When this age was gone, man longed for it. And still today, we wish our bodies were not mortal and that we could live forever. The Bible tells us that because of mankind's sin, we lost immortality and life was no longer perfect. But at that time God promised a Redeemer, the Sacred Promise, who would restore to mankind what sin had taken away.

Jesus taught that if we believe on him we too can have eternal life. Jesus said to her, "I am the resurrection and the life; he who believes in Me will live even if he dies" (John 11:25). He instructed his disciples that "everyone who confesses Me before men, I will also confess him before My Father who is in heaven. But whoever denies Me before men, I will also deny him before My Father who is in heaven" (Matthew 10:32–33).

Christians believe that the Bible reveals God's truth. God's promise of a Redeemer is told by the writers of the Old Testament, and that promise is fulfilled by the death and resurrection of Jesus Christ, as told by the writers of the New Testament. Today, the Christian church continues to spread this story throughout the world.

Afterword

Is the Bible true? Did Jesus Christ die and rise again? Can we see the prediction of the Redeemer in Genesis and then woven through all of history? These are the questions this book has attempted to answer.

From the early middle ages until the eighteenth century, the Christian worldview was dominant in Western civilization. Even before the Christian era, the pagan peoples were devotedly religious, and believed in a large variety of gods who they further believed needed to be worshipped and revered. During the Enlightenment, or Age of Reason, the supernatural was replaced by man's reason, and naturalism began to take precedence over the belief in God. As we move into the twenty-first century, naturalism and humanism have become entrenched in our schools and culture.

According to James Sire in *The Universe Next Door*, naturalism has questioned the belief in miracles, and the historicity of the Bible has been called into question. The Neo-orthodoxy movement of Christianity in the second half of the twentieth century also rejected the miracles of the Bible.[53]

But we can believe the miracles, especially Christ's resurrection. We have tangible evidence, such as Christ's burial shroud, to support our belief. As Paul wrote, "if you confess with your mouth Jesus as Lord, and believe in your heart that God raised Him from the dead, you will be saved" (Romans 10:9).

Starting from the beginning of history, we find the story of man and woman's sin and the expulsion from the Garden of Eden. But mankind is given a promise—a Sacred Promise of a Redeemer who would restore to man the immortality he lost in the "fall." Ancient man wrote that story into the constellations; they wrote it into their myths; they incorporated its ideas into their pagan mystery rites. Seiss explains that even through the darkness of idolatry still shone the true prophetic light.[54]

The ancient reverence which people have always held in regard to the myths of the constellations suggests that they believed they were telling a divine message. Skeptics who wrote that Christianity copied from the pagan myths were, in reality, seeing truths which have flowed from the very beginning of history.

In the constellations we see Virgo with the ear of corn in her hand, showing the idea of the promised Seed. In Libra we see that the promised Seed would come to redeem. The next sign Scorpio shows what the price would be—a conflict with the serpent in which the head of the serpent would be bruised, while the Redeemer would be bruised in the heel. Ophiuchus (Asclepius) and Hercules show in picture form an illustration of Genesis 3:15, the conqueror of the serpent, the Sacred Promise, bringing hope to mankind. The myths also incorporate this idea of a god-man who would struggle with a serpent, representing the evil one.

We have noted the written declarations of a redeemer as we see in Balaam, the prophet from Mesopotamia. Balaam declares, "I see him, but not now; I behold him, but not near; a star shall come forth from Jacob, and a scepter shall rise from Israel" (Numbers 24:17). The great astronomers from Persia recognized a star that signaled the birth of the King of the Jews. This same star is noted among the astronomers of China.

The Sacred Promise has been revealed in history, and the Redeemer has come as a man. He died a cruel death, but his body has been gloriously resurrected. If we believe in him, we too can someday have a resurrected body. We are not lost and hopeless; we are not put in this world without a purpose. We are called to honor God and to do his will. We need to be faithful like Enoch, Noah, and Abraham, who gained approval because they believed things not yet seen (Hebrews 11).

The Story of Christ Told by Matthew

The story of Christ coming to Earth is told in the four biblical gospels: Matthew, Mark, Luke, and John. Each tells the same story, in his own way. Because Matthew was writing to the Jews, he particularly noted how Christ's coming fulfilled prophecies in the Old Testament. The Jews were looking for a messiah to come, but many did not recognize Jesus or accept him, as they were looking for an earthly king. Matthew's story of Christ refers to many Old Testament prophecies.

The book starts with the genealogy of Jesus, tracing his line from Abraham to Joseph, the husband of Mary. After Mary was betrothed to Joseph, but before they "came together," Mary was found to be "with child." Joseph was minded to put her away secretly, but while he thought about these things, an angel of the Lord appeared to him in a dream and said, "Joseph, son of David, do not be afraid to take Mary as your wife; for the Child who has been conceived in her is of the Holy Spirit. She will bear a Son; and you shall call His name Jesus, for He will save His people from their sins" (Matthew 1:20–21).

All this took place that what the prophet had said would be fulfilled, "'Behold, the virgin shall be with child and shall bear a Son, and they shall call His name Immanuel,' which translated means, 'God with us'" (Matthew 1:23; Isaiah 7:14).

After Jesus was born in Bethlehem of Judea, wise men from the east came to Jerusalem, saying they had seen his star in the East and were come to worship him.

Herod was troubled when he spoke with the wise men. He went to the chief priests and scribes to ask where Christ was to be born. And they said, "In Bethlehem of Judea; for this is what has been written by the prophet: 'And you, Bethlehem, land of Judah, are by no means least among the leaders of Judah; for out of you shall come forth a Ruler, who will shepherd My people Israel,'" (Matthew 2:5–6; Micah 5:2).

Herod sent the magi to Bethlehem and told them to come back and let him know when they found the child, so he could worship Him also. The wise men followed the star to where the young child was. They fell down and worshipped him and presented him with gifts—gold, frankincense, and myrrh. When they were warned in a dream not to return to Herod, they returned to their own country.

Then the angel of the Lord appeared to Joseph in a dream saying, "Get up! Take the Child and His mother and flee to Egypt, and remain there until I tell you; for Herod is going to search for the Child to destroy Him." This command fulfilled what was spoken by the Lord through the prophet saying, "Out of Egypt I called My Son" (Matthew 2:13, 15; Hosea 11:1).

When Herod saw that he was deceived by the wise men, he was very angry, and put to death all the male children in Bethlehem from two years old and under. Then was fulfilled what was spoken by Jeremiah the prophet, saying, "A voice was heard in Ramah, weeping and great mourning, Rachel weeping for her children; and she refused to be comforted, because they were no more" (Matthew 2:18; Jeremiah 31:15).

When Herod was dead, Joseph went out of Egypt to return to Judea but was warned by God in a dream to go instead to Nazareth of Galilee. This plan fulfilled what was spoken by the prophets, "He shall be called a Nazarene" (Matthew 2:23).

John the Baptist came preaching in the wilderness of Judea, saying, "Repent, for the kingdom of heaven is at hand." John's appearance is foretold by Isaiah the prophet: "The voice of one crying in the wilderness, 'Make ready the way of the Lord, Make His paths straight!'" (Matthew 3:2–3; Isaiah 40:3).

Jesus came to John the Baptist at the Jordan to be baptized by him; and when he was baptized, he saw the Spirit of God descending on him like a dove. A voice came from heaven saying, "This is My beloved Son, in whom I am well pleased" (Matthew 3:17).

When Jesus was tempted of Satan in the wilderness, Jesus used words from the Old Testament to resist Satan's temptation:

Man shall not live on bread alone, but on every word that proceeds out of the mouth of God. (Matthew 4:4; Deuteronomy 8:3)

You shall not put the LORD your God to the test. (Matthew 4:7; Deuteronomy 6:16)

You shall worship the LORD your God and serve Him only. (Matthew 4:10; Deuteronomy 6:13)

Jesus went from Galilee to Capernaum, which is by the sea, in the regions of Zebulun and Naphtali, that it would be fulfilled what was spoken by Isaiah the prophet, saying, "The land of Zebulun and the land of Naphtali, by the way of the sea, beyond the Jordan, Galilee of the Gentiles—the people who were sitting in darkness saw a great light, and to those who were sitting in the land and shadow of death, upon them a light dawned" (Matthew 4:15–16; Isaiah 9:1–2).

Jesus went about teaching in the synagogues, preaching the gospel of the kingdom and healing all kinds of sicknesses.

In his Sermon on the Mount Jesus presented a high standard of morality which included not judging others and loving our enemies. Jesus said, "Do not think that I came to abolish the Law or the Prophets; I did not come to abolish but to fulfill" (Matthew 5:17).

Jesus went into Peter's house and saw Peter's wife's mother lying sick. He healed her and he also healed those who were demon-possessed. "He cast out the spirits with a word, and healed all who were ill. This was to fulfill what was spoken through Isaiah the prophet: 'He himself took our infirmities, and carried away our diseases'" (Matthew 8:16–17; Isaiah 53:4).

When the Pharisees questioned why Jesus ate with tax gatherers and sinners, Jesus said, "It is not those who are healthy who need a physician, but those who are sick. But go and learn what this means, 'I desire compassion and not sacrifice,' for I did not come to call the righteous, but sinners" (Matthew 9:12–13; Hosea 6:6).

Jesus instructed his twelve disciples with these words before sending them out:

> Therefore everyone who confesses Me before men, I will also confess him before my Father who is in heaven. But whoever denies Me before men, I will also deny him before My Father who is in heaven. Do not think that I came to bring peace on the earth; I did not come to bring peace, but a sword. For I came to set a man against his father, and a daughter against her mother, and a daughter-in-law against her mother-in-law; and a man's enemies will be the members of his household. (Matthew 10:32–36; Micah 7:6)

> And he who does not take his cross and follow after me is not worthy of Me. He who has found his life shall lose it, and he who has lost his life for My sake shall find it. (Matthew 10:38–39)

When John the Baptist heard in prison about the works of Christ, he sent two of his disciples to Christ to ask him, "'Are you the Expected One, or shall we look for someone else?' Jesus answered and said to them, 'Go and report to John what you hear and see: the blind receive sight and the lame walk, the lepers are cleansed and the deaf hear, the dead are raised up, and the poor have the gospel preached to them. And blessed is he who does not take offense at Me'" (Matthew 11:3–6). Then Jesus said regarding John the Baptist, "This is the one about whom it is written, 'Behold, I send My messenger ahead of

You, who will prepare Your way before You'" (Matthew 11:10; Malachi 3:1).

Large multitudes followed Jesus and he healed them all, yet he warned them not to make Him known, that it would fulfill what was spoken by Isaiah the prophet:

> Behold, My Servant whom I have chosen; My Beloved in whom My soul is well-pleased; I will put My Spirit upon Him, and He shall proclaim justice to the Gentiles. He will not quarrel, not cry out; nor will anyone hear His voice in the streets. A battered reed He will not break off, and a smoldering wick He will not put out, until He leads justice to victory. And in His name the Gentiles will hope. (Matthew 12:18–21; Isaiah 42:1–4)

Jesus taught the people in parables:

> Therefore I speak to them in parables; because while seeing they do not see, and while hearing they do not hear, nor do they understand. In their case the prophecy of Isaiah is being fulfilled, which says, "You will keep on hearing, but will not understand; and you will keep on seeing, but will not perceive; for the heart of this people has become dull, with their ears they scarcely hear, and they have closed their eyes, otherwise they would see with their eyes, hear with their ears, and understand with their heart and return, and I would heal them." (Matthew 13:13-15; Isaiah 6:9-10)

Speaking in parables fulfilled what was spoken by the prophet saying, "I will open My mouth in parables; I will utter things hidden since the foundation of the world" (Matthew 13:35; Psalm 78:2).

Then Jesus warned his disciples, "[W]e are going up to Jerusalem; and the Son of Man will be delivered to the chief priests and scribes, and they will condemn Him to death, and will hand Him over to the Gentiles to mock and scourge and crucify Him, and on the third day He will be raised up" (Matthew 20:18–19).

When Jesus and his followers drew near Jerusalem, Jesus sent two disciples to find a donkey tied and a colt with her and to bring them to him. This was done to fulfill what was spoken by the prophet: "Say to the daughter of Zion, 'Behold your King is coming to you, gentle and mounted on a donkey, even on a colt, the foal of a beast of burden'" (Matthew 21:5; Zechariah 9:9).

Jesus rode through Jerusalem on a colt, with the multitude spreading their coats and branches on the road and crying, "Hosanna to the Son of David; blessed is he who comes in the name of the LORD; hosanna in the highest!" (Matthew 21:9; Psalm 118:26).

Jesus went into the temple, and drove out those who bought and sold in the temple and overturned the tables of the money changers. He said, "It is written, 'My house shall be called a house of prayer,' but you are making it a robbers' den" (Matthew 21:13; Isaiah 56:7; Jeremiah 7:11).

When the chief priest and scribes heard the children crying out in the temple and saying, "Hosanna to the Son of David," they were indignant and asked Jesus, "Do you hear what these are saying?" and Jesus said to them, "Yes; have you never read, 'Out of the mouth of infants and nursing babies You have prepared praise for Yourself'?" (Matthew 21:16; Psalm 8:2).

The Jewish leaders questioned Jesus, and Jesus told the parable of the vineyard and the hired help mistreating and killing the messengers of the owner. Then Jesus said to them, "Did you never read in the Scriptures, 'The stone which the builders rejected, this became the chief corner stone; this came about from the Lord, and it is marvelous in our eyes'?" (Matthew 21:42; Psalm 118:22–23).

When questioned by the Sadducees, who did not believe in a resurrection, Jesus told them, "But regarding the resurrection of the dead, have you not read what was spoken to you by God: 'I am the God of Abraham, and the God of Isaac, and the God of Jacob'? He is not the God of the dead but of the living" (Matthew 22:31–32; Exodus 3:6, 15).

When the Pharisees questioned Jesus, asking him which is the great commandment in the law, he said to them, "'You shall love the Lord your God with all your heart, and with all your soul, and with all your mind.' This is the great and foremost commandment. The second is like it, 'You shall love your neighbor as yourself.' On these two commandments depend the whole Law and the Prophets" (Matthew 22:37–40; Deuteronomy 6:5; Leviticus 19:18).

Jesus asked the Pharisees, "What do you think about the Christ, whose son is He?" and the Pharisees answered, "The son of David." Jesus replied, "Then how does David in the Spirit call Him 'Lord,' saying, 'The Lord said to my Lord, "Sit at My right hand, until I put Your enemies beneath thy feet"? If David then calls Him 'Lord,' how is He his son?" (Matthew 22:42–45; Psalm 110:1). No one was able to answer Jesus.

Jesus told some parables about the end of times and encouraged the faithful to be ready. After telling the story of the ten virgins awaiting the bridegroom, he said, "Be on the alert then, for you do not know the day nor the hour" (Matthew 25:13).

After telling more parables regarding the kingdom of heaven, Jesus predicted his own death: "You know that after two days the Passover is coming, and the Son of Man is to be delivered up for crucifixion" (Matthew 26:2).

Then Judas was given thirty pieces of silver by the chief priests as payment for Judas' delivery of Jesus to them. At the Feast of Unleavened Bread shared with his disciples, Jesus instituted what we know as the communion service. Afterward, they went to the Mount of Olives. Jesus told his disciples that they would fall away that night, "for it is written, 'I will strike down the shepherd, and the sheep of the flock shall be scattered'" (Matthew 26:31; Zechariah 13:7).

Jesus prayed in the garden of Gethsemane, and began to be sorrowful and deeply distressed. He came to the disciples and said to them, "Are you still sleeping and resting? Behold, the hour is at hand and the Son of Man is being betrayed into the hands of sinners. Get up, let us be going; behold, the one who betrays Me is at hand!" (Matthew 26:45–46).

Judas then kissed Jesus, betraying him. His enemies came and laid hands on Jesus. The disciples forsook Jesus and fled. Jesus was taken to Caiaphas, the high priest, who asked Jesus, "'[T]ell us if you are Christ, the Son of God.' Jesus said to him, 'You have said it yourself; nevertheless I tell you, hereafter you shall see The Son of Man sitting at the right hand of Power, and coming on the clouds of heaven.' Then the high priest tore his robes and said, 'He has blasphemed!'" (Matthew 26:63–65).

Judas was remorseful. He threw down the thirty pieces of silver in the temple and went and hanged himself. The chief priests took the thirty pieces of silver and gave them for the purchase of a potter's field to bury strangers. This was in fulfillment of the prophet Jeremiah, "And they took the thirty pieces of silver, the price of the one whose price had been set by the sons of Israel; and they gave them for the Potter's Field, as the Lord directed me" (Matthew 27:9–10; Jeremiah 32:6–9).

The chief priests hid their real charge against Jesus—his claim of equality with God—because this charge would not persuade the governor, Pilate, to sentence him to death. Instead, they presented a charge of treason—that Jesus called himself the King of the Jews. That crime would carry the death penalty, for it was a challenge to Roman rule.

Pilate delivered Jesus to be scourged. Then the soldiers put a scarlet robe on Him and a twisted crown of thorns on His head and mocked him, saying, "Hail, King of the Jews!" (Matthew 27:28). They spat on him and struck him on the head. Then they led him away to be crucified. They compelled a man of Cyrene, named Simon, to carry the cross. "And when they had crucified him, they divided up His garments among themselves by casting lots" (Matthew 27:35; Psalm 22:18).

Two robbers were crucified with Him, one on the right and another on the left. The chief priests and others mocked him saying, "He saved others; He cannot save Himself" (Matthew 27:42).

From the sixth hour until the ninth hour, as Jesus hung on the cross, there was darkness over all the land. And about the ninth hour Jesus cried out with a loud voice, saying, "My God, My God, why have You forsaken Me?" (Matthew 27:46; Psalm 22:1). Then Jesus cried out again with a loud voice and yielded up His spirit. And the veil of the temple was torn in two from top to bottom, and the earth quaked, rocks were split, and graves were opened. Many bodies of the saints who had fallen asleep were raised and went into the holy city and appeared to many.

The soldiers who were guarding Jesus feared greatly and said, "Truly this was the Son of God!" (Matthew 27:54).

A rich man from Arimathea named Joseph asked Pilate for the body, and wrapped it in a clean linen cloth and laid it in a new tomb, and rolled a large stone against the opening to the tomb. The Pharisees asked Pilate to secure the tomb, afraid that the disciples might steal his body. Pilate gave them a guard and told them to make it as secure as they knew how.

As the day after the Sabbath began to dawn, Mary Magdalene and the other Mary came to see the tomb.

And behold, a severe earthquake had occurred, for an angel of the Lord descended from heaven and came and rolled away the stone and sat on it. And his appearance was like lightning, and his clothing as white as snow. The guards shook for fear of him and became like dead men. The angel said to the women, "Do not be afraid; for I know that you are looking for Jesus who has been crucified. He is not here, for He has risen, just as He said. Come, see the place where He was lying. Go quickly and tell His disciples that He has risen from the dead; and behold, He is going before you into Galilee, there you will see Him; behold, I have told you."

And they left the tomb quickly with fear and great joy and ran to report it to His disciples. (Matthew 28:2–8)

Endnotes

Chapter 1

1. Charles Ryrie, *The Ryrie Study Bible, New American Standard Translation* (Chicago: Moody Press, 1978), 12.

2. Joseph Farah, *The Gospel in Every Book of the Old Testament* (Washington, DC: World Net Daily Books, 2018), 6.

3. Dr. William R. Cooper, *The Authenticity of the Book of Genesis* (England: Creation Science Movement, 2011), 55.

4. Flavius Josephus, Book I of *The Antiquities of the Jews*, from The Complete Works, translated by William Whiston (Nashville: Thomas Nelson, 1998), 36.

5. Frances Rolleston, *Mazzaroth,* Kessinger Legacy Reprints (Whitefish, MT: Kessinger Publishing, 2010), Part 1, 3.

6. William D. Banks, *The Heavens Declare* (Kirkwood, MO: Impact Books, Inc, 2013), 50.

7. Ibid., 64–73.

Chapter 2

8. *The Epic of Gilgamesh,* translated by Maureen Gallery Kovacs, accessed January 3, 2019, http://ancienttexts.org/library/mesopotamian/gilgamesh/tab9/htm.

9. *The Epic of Gilgamesh*, translated by R. Campbell Thompson, accessed January 3, 2019, http://www.sacred-texts.com/ane/eog.htm (tablets 1–12).

Chapter 3

10. Wolfram von Soden, *The Ancient Orient*, translated by Donald G. Schley (Grand Rapids, MI: William B. Eerdmans Pub. Co, 1994), 249.

11. Robert A. Guisepi and F. Roy Williams, "The Advice of an Akkadian Father to His Son," accessed January 3, 2019, http://history-world.org/advice_of_an_akkadian_father-to.htm.

Chapter 4

12. John Watson, "An Overview of Ancient Egyptian Religion," accessed January 3, 2019, http://www.touregypt.net/featurestories/religion.htm.

13. "Osiris," accessed January 3, 2019, http://www.crystalinks.com/osiris.html.

14. D. James Kennedy, *The Real Meaning of the Zodiac* (Fort Lauderdale, FL: Coral Ridge Ministries, 1997), 102–112.

15. Burton Feldman and Robert D. Richardson, Jr, *The Rise of Modern Mythology 1680–1860* (Bloomington: Indiana University Press, 1972), 70.

Chapter 5

16. Jayaram V., "Hinduism and Buddhism," accessed January 3, 2019, https://hinduwebsite.com/hinduism/h_buddhism.asp

17. George Stanley Faber, *The Origin of Pagan Idolatry*, Vol. I, reprint (Whitefish, MT: Kessinger Publishing LLC, 2015–2018), 443.

Chapter 6

18. Jewish Federation of North America, "The Passover Haggadah: A Guide to the Seder," accessed 7/18/2019. jewishfederation.org/images/uploads/holiday_images/39497.pdf.

19. Farah, *The Gospel in Every Book of the Old Testament*, 205.

20. David Limbaugh, *Finding Jesus in the Old Testament* (Washington, DC: Regnery Publishing, 2015), 15.

21. Ibid., 249–250.

Chapter 7

22. D. James Kennedy, *The Real Meaning of the Zodiac* (Fort Lauderdale, FL: Coral Ridge Ministries, 1997), 97.

23. Joseph A. Seiss, *The Gospel in the Stars*, reprint (New York: Cosimo, 2005), 104–105.

Chapter 8

24. Seiss, *Gospel in the Stars*, 49.

25. David Ulansey, *The Origins of the Mithraic Mysteries* (New York: Oxford University Press, 1989).

26. Michael P. Speidel, "Mithra-Orion: Greek Hero and Roman Army God," accessed January 3, 2019, https://catalog.hathitrust.org/Record/000712863.

Chapter 9

27. Farah, *The Gospel in Every Book of the Old Testament*, 6.

28. Faber, *Origin of Pagan Idolatry*, Vol. III, 624.

29. Henry M. Morris, "When They Saw the Star," accessed January 3, 2019, http://www.icr.org/home/resources/resources_tracts_when theysawthestar.

30. Ibid.

31. Ibid.

Chapter 10

32. Chan Kei Thong, *Finding God in Ancient China* (Grand Rapids, MI: Zondervan, 2009), 313–314. Used by permission of the author.

33. Ibid., 317.

34. Ibid., 318.

35. Ibid., 319.

36. Ibid., 11.

37. Ibid., 22.

38. The Collected Statutes of the Mind Dynasty, quoted in Chan Kei Thong, *Finding God in Ancient China* (Grand Rapids, MI: Zondervan, 2009), 116-145. Used by permission of the author.

39. Ibid.

Chapter 11

40. "Thor," accessed January 3, 2019, http://thenorsegods.com/thor.

Chapter 12

41. Christopher Buck, "Quetzalcoatl, the 'Plumed Serpent'," accessed January 3, 2019, http://bahaiteaching.org/quetzalcoatl-the-plumed-serpent.

42. Marie Trevelyan, "Folk-lore and folk stories of Wales," quoted in "The Fiery Flying Serpent," Genesis Park, accessed January 3, 2019, https://www.genesispark.com/essays/fiery-serpent.

43. Christopher Buck, "Quetzalcoatl, the 'Plumed Serpent'," accessed January 3, 2019, http://babaiteachings.org/quetzalcoatl-the-plumed-serpent.

44. "Quetzalcoatl," accessed January 3, 2019, https://www.britannica.com/topic/Quetzalcoatl.

45. Faber, *The Origin of Pagan Idolatry*, Vol 1, 448.

46. Herodotus, *Historiae,* translated by Henry Clay (London: Henry G. Bohn, 1850).

47. Samuel Bochart, *Hierozoocon: sive, de animalibus sacrae scriptura.* In *Libraria Weidmannia* (Leipsig, Germany, 1793–1796), 215.

Chapter 13

48. Pierre Barbet, *A Doctor at Calvary,* France, 1950, translated by The Earl of Wicklow (Garden City, NY: Image Books, 1963)

49. Dr. John H. Heller, *Report on the Shroud of Turin* (Boston: Houghton Mifflin Co, 1983).

50. Ian Wilson, *The Shroud: Fresh Light on the 2000-Year-Old-Mystery* (London: Bantam Books, 2010).

51. Mark Antonacci, *Test the Shroud: At the Atomic and Molecular Levels* (Ashland, OH: Forefront Pub. Co, 2015).

52. John Jackson and The Turin Shroud Center of Colorado, *The Shroud of Turin: A Critical Summary of Observations, Data, and Hypotheses* (Colorado Springs: The Turin Shroud Center of Colorado, 2017), 97: "Dr. Jackson and his TSC associates, after years of intense research following the completion of the STURP project and coupled with the research findings of an ever-expanding body of Shroud scholars, have come to hold the position that the Shroud of Turin is in fact the burial Shroud of Jesus of Nazareth. Others may judge differently or even suspend judgment. That must be respected, so long as it is recognized that a supportable, intellectual position can be reached only after an honest assessment of the totality of evidence."

Afterword

53. James W. Sire, *The Universe Next Door* (Downers Grove, IL: InterVarsity Press, 2009), 139–143.

54. Seiss, *The Gospel in the Stars*, 44.